ZODIAC

NEWRY

Edited by Simon Harwin

First published in Great Britain in 2002 by
YOUNG WRITERS
Remus House,
Coltsfoot Drive,
Peterborough, PE2 9JX
Telephone (01733) 890066

HB ISBN 0 75433 570 4
SB ISBN 0 75433 571 2

FOREWORD

Young Writers was established in 1991 with the aim of promoting creative writing in children, to make reading and writing poetry fun.

Once again, this year proved to be a tremendous success with over 41,000 entries received nationwide.

The Zodiac competition has shown us the high standard of work and effort that children are capable of today. The competition has given us a vivid insight into the thoughts and experiences of today's younger generation. It is a reflection of the enthusiasm and creativity that teachers have injected into their pupils, and it shines clearly within this anthology.

The task of selecting poems was a difficult one, but nevertheless, an enjoyable experience. We hope you are as pleased with the final selection in *Zodiac Newry* as we are.

CONTENTS

St Mary's High School

Ciara Rafferty	1
Cathy Keenan	2
Tracey Byrne	2
Paula McGahan	3
Gemma Malone	4
Karen Finnegan	4
Dara McCoy	5
Grace Clarke	6
Noleen Mallie	6
Louise McGlade	7
Cheryl Treanor	8
Rosie O'Meara	8
Joanne Smyth	9
Sinead Fegan	9
Frances Campbell	10
Clara Rooney	11
Caoimhe Redmond	12
Ciara McNally	12
Maureen Haughey	13
Bridget Grant	13
Deborah McCorry	14
Sinead Malone	14
Nuala Malone	15
Treise Lively	16
Katrina Morgan	17
Kelly McClorey	18
Seannine Hanna	18
Clara McVeigh	19
Kylie Cahill	20
Jenna McLouglin	20
Christina Williamson	21
Ashley O'Hanlon	22
Grainne Maguire	22
Christine Downey	23
Amanda Duffy	24

Martina O'Hare	24
Michelle O'Keefe	25
Seana Dunne	26
Michaela Devlin	26
Ciara McSherry	27
Sarah Taylor	28
Caroleana McGovern	29
Claire Cahill	30
Natalie Sands	30
Tracy Malone	31
Aine McGreevy	31
Denise Kelly	32
Aine Lambe	34
Jenny Shields	34
Christine Kimbley	35
Mary Dixon	35
Aisling Treanor	36
Claire O'Hare	36
Lindsey McLoughlin	37
Christine Taylor	37
Kelly-Louise Franks	38
Michelle Rice	38
Duana Rooney	39
Andrea McGovern	40
Olivia Powell	41
Elaine Byrne	42
Amy McDonnell	42
Karen Convery	43
Sinead McGrath	43
Shaunna Ferns	44
Ciara Mooney	44
Natasha McDonald	45
Linda McGarry	45
Sheila Meagher	46
Marie Claire McAteer	46
Aine Larkin	47
Roisin Lennon	48
Aine McEvoy	48

Deirbhle O'Brien   49
Clare McShane   50
Adele Sarsfield   51
Cassie Kelly   52
Marian McConville   53
Catherine McArdle   53

St Paul's High School
Sean Trainor   54
Darren McCann   55
David Hughes   56
Christopher Cranney   57
Kelly McGurk   58
Orlagh Boyle   58
Lauren O'Grady   59
Jennifer Hughes   60
Thomas Casey   60
Feilin Quinn   61
Danielle Lynch   62
Amanda McTaggart   62
Vanessa McParland   63
Gavin Magee   64
Clare McCann   65
Kevin McQuade   66
Stephen O'Brien   66
Louise Mullan   67
Paula Keenan   67
Eimear Bagnall   68
Ciara Grant   69
Michelle Cunningham   70
Charlene Carlon   71
Catherine Hollywood   72
Sharon Toal   73
Padraig Rogers   74
Sarah McIntyre   74
Caolan McKeown   75
Danielle Brady   75
Denise Leonard   76

Decland Byrne	77
Eva Woods	78
Jennifer Smyth	79
Noleen Carragher	80
Christopher Fearon	80
Lisa Daly	81

Sacred Heart Grammar School

Lisa Fitzgerald	82
Rebecca O'Hare	82
Sarah Jane Quinn	83
Marguerite Sherry	84
Deirdre Rocks	84
Aoife Treanor	85
Cristin Ruddy	86
Marianna McParland	87
Helen McAteer	88
Kellie Rogers	88
Nicole Curran	89
Rosanna Moore	90
Megan Duffy	91
Tina Greenan	92
Aisling Hollowood	92
Sinead Gorman	93
Aisling Walls	94
Margaret Linsey Murray	94
Ciara Ryan	95
Catherine Sherry	95
Jennifer Smith	96
Karen Doran	97
Judy Black	98
Rosaleen McConville	98
Joanne Reid	99
Anne Gallagher	100
Ciara McShane	100
Eve Mallon	101
Sorcha McCaughley	101
Lisa Kelly	102

Chantal Parsons	102
Ann Jennings	103
Siamsa McDonald	103
Niamh McCaughey	104
Ruth Quinn	105
Jane Rooney	106
Bronagh McNally	106
Emer McGowan	107
Cara McCullough	108
Teresa McCabe	108
Keri Fitzpatrick	109
Emer Tumilty	110
Siofra Crozier	111
Louise Byrnes	111
Aoife McCoy	112
Ciara McKeown	112
Leanne McCoy	113
Kerri Coopler	114
Emma McAteer	114
Billie Phipps-Tyndall	115
Lana Mallon	116
Ciara Hughes	117
Janelle McAteer	117
Anna Burke	118
Bronagh Clarke	118
Cathy Grant	119
Claire McMurray	119
Patrice Byrnes	120
Áine Reilly	120
Shellie McKeown	121
Emma O'Gorman	122
Sarah Connolly	122
Nikki Larkin	123
Corinne Jordan	123
Katie McGovern	124
Niamh D'Arcy	124
Sarah-Louise O'Hare	125
Vicki Lennon	125

Saah Gravey	126
Ciara Higgins	126
Claire McAteer	127
Kelly Savage	127
Siofra Gough	128
Ruth Graham	128
Clare Grant	129
Róisín Murphy	130
Lisa Hamill	130
Lucy O'Hare	131
Adele Cunningham	131
Delia Paxton	132
Jennifer Maguire	132
Cecilia McSweeney	133
Leah McGuinness	133
Tara Crilly	134
Claire O'Donnell	134
Naoise Curran	135
Helen McAvoy	136
Carol Duffy	137
Laura Fitzpatrick	137
Shóna McConville	138
Claudia Cole	138
Éadaoin Hynes	139
Ciara Monaghan	139
Emma Madine	140
Bronagh Fitzpatrick	140
Niamh Montgomery	141
Sarah Casey	142
Shauna Reeves	142
Fionnuala Haughey	143
Maria Dobbin	144
Rachel Gribben	144
Siobhan Ruck	145
Amy Lavery	146
Keren Larkin	146
Catherine Hughes	147
Alana Carroll	147

Claire Rooney   148
Elizabeth O'Hanlon   149
Clare Campbell   149
Dominique French   150
Nicola McNally   150
Caitriona Gormley   151
Claire Malone   152
Cathy McAlinden   152
Louise O'Hanlon   153
Grace Cole   153
Niamh Haughey   154
Alannah White   154
Danielle Rooney   155
Yvonne Smyth   156
Nicola Mullan   156
Teresa Quinn   157
Ruth Morris   158
Claire Durkan   159
Jaimie Bishop   160
Susan Cull   161
Caoimhe Quinn   161
Aoibheann Doyle   162
Niamh McCartan   162
Jane Doran   163
Ciara Tumilty   163
Gemma Small   164
Mairead Duffy   164

The Poems

CENTURIES OF PEOPLE

The 50s people wore different clothes,
Full colourful skirts with small and big shirts,
It was a bit like Grease
Except for Danny and Sandy.

In the 60s they wore nifty clothes,
The girls wore hot pants and short skirts,
Then there were the boys who were girls' toys,
This is all that happened in the sixties.

The 70s people are hippies,
They used only the peace sign,
They were into saving trees,
For example, pine,
They wore bell bottoms and bright tops,
This best describes the seventies.

Well in the 80s what can I say?
Their clothes were never here to stay,
With their tartan skirts and their stripy tights,
Oh please give me a bucket or I won't be nice.

In the 90s their clothes were OK
There's nothing I can really say.

Oh yes there is something else I have to say
I'm glad we're in the New Century,
Party, we're in the New Century.

Ciara Rafferty (12)
St Mary's High School

A CHRISTMAS FRIGHT ON CHRISTMAS NIGHT

It was about two Christmases ago,
The ground was thick with snow,
I was so excited about Christmas Day,
I had asked for a pottery set with clay.

I could not sleep, I was twisting and turning,
I had a picture in my head of Santa
Coming down the chimney and burning.

I was restless all of that night,
So I went do downstairs and I got a fright,
I saw my daddy laying out presents for me,
He was doing it quietly putting them
Under the Christmas tree.

I cried and cried for days on end,
But my broken heart would never mend,
So from that day on, I wondered why
Santa wasn't there and every night it
Would make me cry.

I didn't know who to blame
But Christmas after that would
Never be the same.

Cathy Keenan (13)
St Mary's High School

MY FANTASY LAND

The snow would glisten on the ground,
Like a blanket of white covering the land,
The bare, brown hands coming from beneath
And are sleeping and as I shiver I
Have a warm feeling inside.

As the snowmen stand alone with their
Scarves blowing in the wind, they don't
Move or make a sound, I stand beside
The sleeping bed of roses and feel so proud.

Tracey Byrne (12)
St Mary's High School

AUTUMN

Three months of colour,
Three months of crunching and rustling of leaves,
Three months of slapping and tinkling rain,
Three months of autumn.

Squirrels running up and down trees,
Badgers nesting under leaves,
Birds resting on telephone wires,
Trees covered with red, orange fires.

The sky is grey with a shimmering sun,
Children playing and having fun,
Yellow, red, orange and brown,
Leaves are blowing all around town.

Just three months of a beautiful season,
Short as a flash and I see no reason,
Why people should be gloomy and sad,
When artists and naturalists are glad.

Three months of colour,
Three months of crunching and rustling of leaves,
Three months of slapping and tinkling of rain,
Three months of autumn.

Paula McGahan (13)
St Mary's High School

WHAT HAPPENS TO MY TOYS AT NIGHT

Mum what happens to my toys at night,
When I turn off my bedroom light?
I often hear strange noises Mum
To get to sleep, I convince myself, it's my tum.

Last night they talked to me Mum
Toys talking to me, I felt so dumb,
It was the soldiers, Mum telling me what to do,
This morning I woke up and I ran straight to the loo.

I'm afraid to go to bed tonight Mum
I know they're going to run wild round my room,
Then there's the dolls Mum
They just like having great fun.

It's not fair on me Mum
Don't you see the big brown bear in the corner,
I was so sad today Mum, people were calling me names
And left me out of all their games.

So Mum what happens to my toys at night
When I turn off my bedroom light?
Help me Mum, help me find out,
What my toys really get up to
In the middle of the night.

Gemma Malone (13)
St Mary's High School

WHAT IF

What if the world was no longer round?
What if we all walked upside down?
What if we had wings to fly?
What if we could touch the sky?
What if dogs were pink and blue?
And birds could talk like me and you?

What if money grew on trees?
And the family pet was a buzzing bee?
What if school was no such thing?
What if the only lessons learned was to dance and sing?
What if these things really did come true?
In such a colourful world
We'd never feel blue.

Karen Finnegan (12)
St Mary's High School

I JUST LOVE MY SISTER

I have a sister,
Who gets on my nerves,
She fights with me
And even bites me.

The thing that I hate most about her,
Is that she is smart and devious.

I get on her nerves too,
Because I am the same size as her,
But that's good because I am quite tall
And she's just plain, old small.

My mammy goes crazy when she sees us fighting
And says she is going to squash us like peas.

But if we keep quarrelling and barrelling,
Like a tape going backwards and forwards.

But in the end she just leaves on holidays with my dad too
And my poor old auntie Kate has to suffer again!

Dara McCoy (11)
St Mary's High School

THERE IS NO SANTA CLAUS

One day while sitting on the grass,
My friends marched up as bold as brass.
We think there's something you should know,
Then moving close and bending low,
They start to speak and then a pause,
There's no such thing as Santa Claus.

The news hit me like a bolt out of the blue,
In shock I didn't know what to do,
Should I act cool, should I act calm,
Pretend I didn't give a damn?
When all the time inside my head - poof!
The magic of Christmas was dead.

The sleigh swooshing across the sky,
Santa's hot milk and hot pie,
The clatter of reindeers' hooves,
As they wait patiently on the roofs,
In a flash they destroyed the magic,
No more Santa Claus, oh, it's tragic!

Grace Clarke (14)
St Mary's High School

MY TRIP TO THE CAVES

We're off to Fermanagh,
Away we go,
To see the caves way down below,
We're finally here, wha-ha, wha-ha.

Down in the caves,
So quiet and cold,
To see the things,
Which have yet to be shown.

There's stalagmites
And stalactites,
Which grew over one million years ago
And the porridge pot which overflowed.

We're back on the bus,
Where there's such a rush,
Just to get home before the minibus.

Noleen Mallie (13)
St Mary's High School

BALING

The time of year came for the fields to be baled
The weather needed to be good
And so far my father had not been failed.

Woken by the constant buzzing of the machines,
The chopping of the clean blades whipping
Through the fresh grass,
The hiss and the click when it stops,
Out comes the bales with a thump.

From the middle strung out like a Swiss roll,
With lemon curd as its filling,
The wet glittered gracefully on the bale
An urge to jump on it but was I willing?

The wrappers came next to coat the bale,
Layers upon layers of silky stretchy material,
Wrapped it up like a leather dress.

As the machines disappear, and the bales are drawn,
The place goes quiet for another year.

Louise McGlade (13)
St Mary's High School

THE BATTLE OF LIGHT OVER DARK (AN OPEN FIRE)

I can see little fingers reaching out of the dark,
Jumping and leaping as high as they can,
Out of the darkness more come to play,
Until at last we have our display.

All of a sudden we see the shapes,
A tree, a house,
Look a car trying to escape,
The darkness is fading,
The light grows strong.

Soon we can see only light,
Orange and yellow scream with delight,
The flames of the fire have won,
At last, the heat reaches out to us
And shares its warmth.

Cheryl Treanor (13)
St Mary's High School

MY POEM

A hairy monster
A fearsome beast
Who knows what lies in his lair beneath?
Who is his master?
A witch, ha, ha, ha! A goblin, he, he, he!
Two bulging red eyes!
Two rosy cheeks
Who or whatever it is should be locked up
And never released!

Rosie O'Meara (11)
St Mary's High School

DON'T

Don't tell me what to do,
I am a teenager!
Don't tell me to clean it up,
I am not your slave!
Don't tell me to tidy my room,
I am growing up!
Don't tell me I can't go,
I am not a child!
Don't you dare call me your wee baby,
I am out of nappies!
Don't you think of embarrassing me,
I am ashamed!
Don't you think of answering me back,
I am your daughter!

Joanne Smyth (14)
St Mary's High School

MY MUM

Wash those dishes,
Make your bed,
That's what my mum says
She's not right in the head.

Take the washing out,
Pick up those toys,
But Mum, but Mum, they're not mine
They're the boys'.

Despite what I've said,
She's really, really kind,
So although I have to do my chores,
I really don't mind.

Sinead Fegan (12)
St Mary's High School

THE LITTLE OLD MAN WITH THE GOLDEN JAW

Down by the lake beside the haunted house there
Lives an old man with a golden jaw.

He lives in a cave that's damp and gloomy,
Only a shimmer of light penetrating the cracks
In the rocks on the cave's roof.

For he is the little old man with the golden jaw.

He's more like a monster than a little old man.

He has a long, pointy nose and a huge red pimple,
He also has two very small feet with two tiny shoes for them.

For he is the little old man with the golden jaw.

When he puts his clothes on they are the same every day.

He wears a pair of tattered brown trousers with a belt,
He wears a musty white T-shirt.

For he is the little old man with the golden jaw.

He goes out in his boat every morning at six,
So he can catch some fish for his new breakfast diet.

His boat is a pale colour with patches of seaweed stuck to it.

His is now called the little old man with the golden tooth
For a very simple reason.

He ventures out one cold and foggy morning to
Catch some fish for his breakfast.
But the hook of his fishing line was wrapped around
His front left tooth,
As he cast the line into the lake,
Out popped his tooth.

Instead he now shows a tooth made of gold.

For he is now the little old man with the golden tooth
And the golden jaw.

Frances Campbell (13)
St Mary's High School

LOST LOVED ONES

When I saw you lying there in the coffin,
I felt so empty, so alone like I was the only one there.
You were as pale as snow on a cold winter's day,
I cried for hours wishing you were still with us
Making us laugh.

I couldn't believe you had gone, just went from this world,
Like a light bulb that had just been switched off,
There were candles around you making you seem so peaceful,
That helped me a lot.

I wish you were still with us giggling along with everyone,
Making dinner, slicing food like you always did.
Every Saturday you got your hair done,
You always had nice, thick hair, I loved you so much.

But now I'll never see you again,
I know you are with me in spirit wherever I go,
I will feel you in the air,
In the breeze through my hair.

Clara Rooney (13)
St Mary's High School

DON'T!

Don't touch that cat it will give you fleas
And don't roll on the grass,
You'll dirty your knees.

Don't touch my car, it's only new
And put on your socks or you'll
Catch the flu.

Don't eat that bar before your tea,
Or you'll ruin your appetite you see.

Don't hit your brother or I'll hit you
And stop jumping on the furniture or
I'll put you black and blue.

Don't eat those sweets before you go to bed
Or every tooth will rot in your head.

Caoimhe Redmond (12)
St Mary's High School

MY SISTER LUCY

My sister Lucy, she is such a pain,
All she ever does is blabber and
She drives me insane.

When she is sleeping, she looks so cute,
But when she is not, she looks like a boot.

She nags at me to let her see,
Whatever it is to be.

She shouts and screams all over the house,
Until she gets it makes you fret!

Ciara McNally (12)
St Mary's High School

THUNDER

Sometimes I sit and wonder,
Why God invented thunder,
Is he cross? Is he mad?
My nephew thinks he's been bad.

As I look up to the sky,
I hear the dog outside cry,
As lightning strikes in the night,
Sometimes it gives us a fearful fright.

So God please tell me why,
Lightning appears in the sky,
It's getting closer by the hour,
The safest place is in your car.

Maureen Haughey (11)
St Mary's High School

IN MY WORLD

The lights will be glistening
And everyone listening,
To the true Santa talking with glee,
He will tell us the truth that
Everyone's lying and Santa
Really is he,
Word will be spread
And even be read,
That Santa is alive and true
And old Father Christmas
Will have joy in meeting us,
On December the 25th.

Bridget Grant (13)
St Mary's High School

CHILDHOOD DREAMS

It was mid-autumn
The ground carpeted with crispy leaves,
Brown as conkers, red as fire,
Scattered beside the fence of barbed wire.
Over the fence and to the field,
Climbing the conker tree to collect our yield.
Then the roller coaster a dirt laden track,
Now smothered in leaves,
We started from the top a rocky, slanted hill,
Me and my friends went running down,
It gave us such a thrill!
Up and down, round and round,
Your feet could barely touch the ground,
Years rolled on, I'm thirteen now
'A typical teen',
Across the field I see no more green,
Only diggers and noisy machines,
Chewing up my childhood dreams.

Deborah McCorry (13)
St Mary's High School

THE FEELING

The wind was howling
And the trees were rustling,
It was a cold, autumn day.
We were snuggled up in
Our cosy coats.

As we were walking down the path,
The cold wind hit our faces like waves of icy breath.
Leaves were swirling everywhere, brushing through
Our hair as they passed.

Animals getting ready to hibernate,
Birds singing their goodbye songs,
As I walked down the path,
It was bleak, not a soul in sight.

Sinead Malone (13)
St Mary's High School

HALLOWE'EN NIGHT

The night fell dark so quickly
The moon shone brightly,
We put on our hats,
We began to chase the cats.

We played 'Trick or Treat',
And asked for a sweet,
While the leaves blew around,
We heard nothing, not even a sound.

With pumpkins, hats and masks,
We got all sorts of tasks,
Then we heard a mouse squeak,
And we all did freak.

We jumped through the ditch
While followed by a witch,
We played another game
And eleven-thirty came.

The stars were all out as we played
They shone with a beautiful display,
It was the best Hallowe'en ever
Because I was very clever.

Nuala Malone (11)
St Mary's High School

A DISAPPOINTMENT

It was early Christmas morning
And I could hardly wait,
I had to yawn but couldn't
For fear I might be late.

I walked the hall like a tightrope,
The slightest sound and I'm caught,
I reached my destination,
But found the door was taut.

My heart racing, but I did it,
I'm finally going to meet him,
I'm going to meet Santa Claus
After all these years of waiting!

I tried the door again
And pushed it ajar,
To find to my disappointment,
I'd missed my shining star.

At dinner that evening,
I told them of my adventure,
That I had caught Mr Santa Claus,
Well nearly, he was far too clever!

It was on one Saturday morning,
I lay down on Mum's bed,
I asked her about Santa Claus,
I was very confused in my head.

It was then that I found out,
I was a little upset,
Christmas will never be the same again,
I liked to sneak about.

And so there's my disappointment,
You probably felt the same,
Although a little of me still believes
And Santa Claus I'll claim!

Treise Lively (13)
St Mary's High School

NO MORE MAGIC

Christmas Eve finally came,
I was so excited,
My brother was the same.

That night in bed
Lots of things went
Through my head.

To me Santa was magic,
Going around the world
In one night.

People always said they
Heard Santa on the roof.
I never believed them
And now I had proof.

That night I heard Mum
And Dad turn on the
Living room light,
The magic wasn't there
Anymore, from now
On Christmas was going
To be a bore.

Katrina Morgan (13)
St Mary's High School

TRAGEDY STRIKES THE BIG APPLE

Crash
The first plane hits,
People screaming like banshees,
Running in circles like a hamster
Running in its wheel.

Crash
The second plane hits
The building on fire
Smoke bellowing out of it
Like a volcano that just erupted,
People jumping out the windows
Trying to save their lives,
Both buildings come down like dominoes,
People coming out of the smoke like ghosts,
Terror in the streets as the World
Trade Centre comes down.

Kelly McClorey (12)
St Mary's High School

SOMEONE VERY SPECIAL

He has been there,
He was always somewhere,
No matter where I go,
I know he's there.

He took me places,
Places I never knew before,
It seems as if he wasn't gone,
He is still present to us.

The someone special in my life,
Is my dad,
The best dad there could ever be,
I don't know where I would be now.

Today I am lost without him,
But I know there is a part of me,
Will never forget him,
That part of me is my heart.

Seannine Hanna (14)
St Mary's High School

NEW YORK

Another day of pain and suffering,
Do you know when it will end?
Will our lives ever be the same
And will the danger fade that is lurking ahead?

Do you know what two planes did to New York?
Did you see and did you talk?
Did your mind think of the worst?
Or did you unexpectedly weep?
Did you know that the people died?
Or did you pray they would survive?

Did you ever feel such pain?
And do you wish your friends
And family were alive?
Just to say your goodbyes!

Clara McVeigh (12)
St Mary's High School

SCHOOL

The corridor is long and bright,
The windows each side let in the light,
Standing here amongst this silence (which is very rare),
I stand at these windows and outside I glare.
It's not a good day, I think the rain is falling,
And somewhere in the distance birds are calling.
Above the wall I see umbrellas as people hurry past,
And wonder if this rainy day is really going to last.
I smell smoke from chimneys mixed with the smell of food,
It must be getting near dinner time so that is something good.

Outside around the school I start walking,
I hear people's voices and see dinner ladies talking,
I hear cars swishing by and some going slow,
Is this rain going to last? I just don't know.
Then I sigh and think, 'What the hell?'
I have to go in 'cause I hear the bell.

Kylie Cahill (13)
St Mary's High School

THE COLD

I woke up one day
With a tickle in my nose,
I sneezed all that day
Till my face turned like a rose.

I didn't sleep that night
With a tickle in my throat,
I coughed all that night
Then I looked like a goat.

I woke up today
With no tickle at all,
Now that I was fit today
I have to go and play.

Jenna McLoughlin (12)
St Mary's High School

GONE, BUT NOT FORGOTTEN

I waited endlessly and sadly at the bedside for the news to be told.

My aunt arranging the still, cold room,
With flickering candles, and sighing.

At five o'clock, my father and aunt followed,
Carrying the box to the small quiet home.

Relatives and strangers entered silently,
Sitting, praying and staring sadly at what lay so very still.

Florists came with the colourful arrangements,
Carpeting the naked, cold hall.

Hustle and chatter, teacups clashing,
Smiles and tears, people dashing.

Family just near, as silence falls,
Beneath us lies, a woman once tall.

My great grandma, whom I loved so much,
Not present,
But my memories, always in touch.

Christina Williamson (14)
St Mary's High School

SCHOOL TIME

When I went to go to school,
Walking down as if I was cool,
Then I realised I was late.

The teacher told me,
To tell me the truth
And not to make up a silly excuse.

I saw a man dead,
I had a sore leg,
I couldn't walk fast
But I made it here at last.

Next time you're late,
It will come to your fate,
You'll work hard at school
And stop acting like a fool.

Ashley O'Hanlon (13)
St Mary's High School

A RAINY DAY

I stood at the window,
The rain poured down,
It ran like a river down
The steep hill,
Nothing stood in its way,
It pushed leaves and
Pebbles out of its path.

My gaze then changed as
I watched another river,
It was a raindrop
On the window as it
Found its path down
The pane of glass.

Although on a rainy day,
It is dark and dull,
But the ground is full
Of new life that needs to grow,
They will only grow with
Plenty of rain.

Grainne Maguire (13)
St Mary's High School

WEATHER

The weather today is wet and cold,
Just like the weather forecast has told.
People dressed up warm and ready for school,
They do not want to look like a fool.
Drip, drop, the rain falls down,
People shivering all around.

The bell rings with a great big roar,
Lots of people running through the door.
In the class it's warm and dry,
The teacher says, 'Look at that sky.'
Ten o'clock the sun comes out,
The teacher gives a very big shout.

The bell rings, it's time to go,
Now the sun is down very low.
The sound now is drip, drop, drip, drop,
It starts all over again - will it ever stop?

Christine Downey (12)
St Mary's High School

REMEMBERING

The old woman sat in her rocking chair
Thinking of days gone by,
She remembered her childhood, a wonderful time,
Now all she could do was sigh.

She thought of the time when she was a girl,
She was beautiful and fair.
She could picture herself in a long, flowing dress,
With her lovely, long, blonde hair.

Now age had crept upon her,
And her beautiful hair was now grey,
Her lovely fair skin had withered with age,
And her body was weakening each day.

Those memories had all come flooding back,
But she was no longer sad,
The old woman was happy for
The wonderful life she had had.

Amanda Duffy (11)
St Mary's High School

TEENY-WEENY DEIDRE

Teeny-weeny Deidre
Is a teeny-weeny freak
With her teeny-weeny hands
And teeny-weeny feet.

Teeny-weeny Deidre
Is a teeny-weeny geek
With teeny-weeny eyes
And teeny-weeny teeth.

With a teeny-weeny nose
And a teeny-weeny mouth,
Teeny-weeny Deidre
Is the best friend about.

Martina O'Hare (12)
St Mary's High School

THE ZOO

My first trip to the zoo was when I was eight,
I was so excited, I just couldn't wait.

Mum made a picnic while Dad packed the car,
Me and my brother hoped it would not be far.

Everything was done, we were ready to go,
Gavin told Dad not to drive too slow.

We got to the zoo and queued at the gate,
Everyone wound as tight as springs,
We just couldn't wait.

Dad shouted 'Hold on,'
As Mum grabbed some snacks,
'Honestly Michelle you're like a jack-in-the-box.'

The chimps were busy chattering,
The camel chewing his cud
And slimy Sid, the six foot snake
Was bathing in the sun.

We slept like logs the whole way home,
Strapped safely in the car,
I opened my eyes, we pulled into the drive
And said, 'That wasn't very far.'

Michelle O'Keefe (13)
St Mary's High School

THE DAY THAT CHANGED OUR LIVES

Tuesday the eleventh,
Everything was fine,
Till one fifty-eight, why that time?
The Twin Towers were standing, but not for long,
At three thirty-seven, they were gone.

People were working, getting on with their lives,
While a plane was hijacked with a set of knives,
The people aboard were told to phone home to say goodbye
And that they were going to die.

Two planes crashed into the Twin Towers,
Black smoke filled the air,
But the terrorists did not care,
People started running for their lives,
The dead and the injured did not make a pretty sight.

People were trapped and knew they would die,
While others would watch and just cry,
Some jumped out of the windows from a high floor,
When they did they knew they wouldn't live much more.

Thousands died, thousands are missing,
It is all over the news and radio for you to listen to,
America will never be the same,
The people who did it should live in shame.

Seana Dunne (13)
St Mary's High School

HALLOWE'EN

Hallowe'en is coming
the nights get very dark.
There's an eerie, eerie feeling
as you walk alone in the park.

The sky is very colourful,
the bonfire spits out blazes,
the children have fun and laughter
at all the scary faces.

Michaela Devlin (11)
St Mary's High School

THE FOUR SEASONS

Spring brings new life to the trees,
the plants, the flowers and the busy bees.
The grass is growing and the lawns need cutting,
another few weeks and the schools will be shutting!

Summer is a season full of sun,
when we laugh and play and have great fun.
We don't even have to go to school,
we can laze about or play in the pool.

The first sign of autumn is the falling leaves,
it's not as warm and there are fewer bees.
The Hallowe'en bonfires are alight,
and the evenings are not as bright.

Our fingers and toes are feeling numb,
we know now that winter has come.
It's dark and dreary, cold and wet,
those long summer days we soon forget.

Ciara McSherry (11)
St Mary's High School

CONFUSION

Oh no I'm late!
Don't hesitate
I've lost my sock and
Can't open the lock.
What shall I do?
Mum's just caught the flu.

I've lost my sheet of writing
It's probably what the dog's biting,
Oh Molly's crying
Well at least Dad's started frying,
All the breakfast for the little terrors
Otherwise they'd be beggars.

I've opened the lock and
Found my sock
It wasn't under my bed
It was in the shed
Oh I've got a sore head.

I'm ready to go
Before I explode,
The noise I hear
Oh yes, the bus is here.
Thank God, I got out of that house
I'll bet you there will be no sound
But a little mouse.

At least I got to school at nine
So I didn't have to pay the fine!

Sarah Taylor (13)
St Mary's High School

MY GRANDAD

He was small and plump with black hair and glasses,
He had rosy red cheeks and a lovely smile,
He was always really kind.

He loved all children and pets,
And he never passed judgement,
He treated everyone with respect,
And just expected respect back.

But then out of the blue, he had a heart attack,
He recovered, but was told he would have to lose
Weight for a pacemaker,
But not long after he had another,
It was a day before his birthday.

He came around, or so we thought,
About twenty minutes after,
He was laughing and joking then,
He died.

I cried, I wondered why, why him?
I stopped and froze, waiting,
Hoping he would come back like before,
But he never did.

He died on his birthday which is 7th October
I miss him very much,
And wish he would come back.

Caroleana McGovern (12)
St Mary's High School

WHAT IF?

What if the world was
Turned upside down,
So that clouds were
On the ground and
Buildings floated in the sky?

What if birds couldn't fly
And the grass wasn't green?
What if people couldn't walk
And dogs weren't seen?
What if this poem went on
Forever?

What if?

Claire Cahill (14)
St Mary's High School

WHY?

People scared from seeing buildings fall,
Waving white flags for help,
No one can save them,
They're thinking they're going to die
And leaving all their families behind.

Why do they do this?
They should be ashamed of themselves,
They should tell the world what they have done,
Why did they want these people dead?
They have done nothing wrong,
Hope it doesn't start World War 3,
All we can do now is pray.

Natalie Sands (12)
St Mary's High School

WORMS

When the earth is turned in spring,
The worms are fat as anything.
The birds come flying around
And eat them right off the ground.
They like worms just as I,
Like bread, milk and apple pie.

Once, when I was just young
I put a worm upon my tongue.
I didn't like the taste of it,
So I did not swallow it.

But oh, it makes my mother squirm
Because she thinks I ate the worm.

Tracy Malone (12)
St Mary's High School

THE PEACE MAN

Have you ever seen the peace man
And his beautiful silver coat?
Have you ever seen his small round face
Or his beautiful peace boat?

No you've never seen the peace man
And I shall tell you why.
You are the one that causes war
And makes the people cry.

So be quiet, hush, be calm
Because someone is watching.
He is the peace man.

Aine McGreevy (12)
St Mary's High School

WHY!

Why did it happen?
What did we do?
This terrible day
Brought something new.

Why did it happen?
What can I say?
This terrible crime
Leaves us in dismay.

Why did it happen?
God I feel so sad,
I cannot believe
Someone can be so bad.

Why did it happen?
These people out there,
Petrified and dying, don't they care?

Why did it happen?
Now thousands are dead,
I shudder to think
What went through their heads!

Why did it happen?
Are people insane?
To deliberately kill
By crashing a plane.

Why did it happen?
Those people most ask
As they search throw the rubble
What a terrible task.

Why did it happen?
So many will die,
As we watch in horror
I see my mum cry.

Why did it happen?
They must have been scared
To jump out of windows
And die on the kerbs.

Why did it happen?
I will never forget,
The cries of people
On my TV set.

Why did it happen?
As we look in horror
The building's collapsing
I fear for tomorrow.

Why did it happen?
We all have to pray,
To help the firefighters
As they meet each day.

Why did it happen?
As we see people cry
And the ambulance people
See so many die.

Why did it happen?
September the 11th,
As people went on their way.

Why did it happen?
I just want to cry
And as those wicked people,
Why? Why? Why?

Denise Kelly (13)
St Mary's High School

SCHOOL WEEK

Monday, what a shame
Time to start the week again!

Tuesday, not much better
In English we wrote a boring letter.

Wednesday was quite a bore
Maths, I'm sure people could hear me snore!

Thursday, one day to Friday
Wouldn't you know
The day would have to go so slow!

Friday thank God it's here
Weekend will probably fly
The dreaded Monday draws near.

Monday, what a shame
Time to start the week again!

Aine Lambe (12)
St Mary's High School

CHRISTMAS

The tree has now gone up
The angel sits on the top
Everything is in place
Apart from my parents, who shop in a race.

At night the lights go on
Whilst Phil Coulter sings a song
It brings a smile to my face
And happiness in our home place.

Jenny Shields (13)
St Mary's High School

JUST LISTEN

I am not just a child,
I have lots to say,
I could tell an adult about what's happening,
In the world today.

I know you don't believe me,
Many have told me so,
But every time,
I try to prove you wrong,
You don't want to know.

So remember, just listen,
To what we have to say,
Then you grown ups,
Will have a peaceful day.

Christine Kimbley (13)
St Mary's High School

ANIMAL PAIN

There is a young girl called Mary.
She loves animals ever so much.
Four dogs and a cat she has
But to have a rabbit is her wish.
Maybe she could even have a fish.
Mary's heart is broken when she
Hears the news reporter say
'Animals hurt by fireworks.'

Mary Dixon (12)
St Mary's High School

LOVE HURTS

I met a boy for the first time
I looked straight at him, suddenly he turned and stared at me
And finally I let my heart go free.

He was the first boy to notice me,
Then he started to talk,
My mind was saying say it, say it,
I only wanted to tell him how I felt.

Every day that I see him,
I'll love him a little more and when I love him a little more,
My heart will grow a little more sore,
It is so sore cos I love him so much,
It is like a stab to my heart with a knife,
But I'll still love that little bit more each day,
Until something bad flows my way
And then we'll part for life.

Aisling Treanor (14)
St Mary's High School

MY WEE DOG

My wee dog had very long hair,
One day I awoke to find her bare.
Off I went to the vet,
He said, 'Oh this is quite rare!'
One week later it started to grow
And her hair colour was fair!

Claire O'Hare (11)
St Mary's High School

DON'T DARE!

'Don't dare' is what I hear,
Nagging in my ear,
Every time I want to do
Something I'd like to.

'Don't dare' is a warning
Which I hear when I wake in the morning,
When I go to school,
So I won't act like a ridiculous fool.

'Don't dare' is a rhyme
Which I'm told all the time,
When I want to go somewhere
I get the 'don't dare' threatening glare.

Lindsey McLoughlin (14)
St Mary's High School

ABORTION

I don't want to die
Please don't let me
I have done nothing wrong
Only want someone who loves me.

I have little toes and fingers
I have started to kick
Only you are the one
Who will be throwing me away.

Please don't kill me
I will love you
Will you love me?

Christine Taylor (14)
St Mary's High School

SENSES

I see birds flying in the sky,
Fast cars go flying by.
I see trees blowing in the breeze,
Is that the rattle of John's keys?
I see rubbish in front of the school,
I wonder who is breaking the rules.

I hear teachers talking to their class,
Working hard, exams to pass.
The rain has started, umbrellas I see,
I see people smoking, how stupid can they be.
The smell of food, it's lunch time you see,
Classes over for the morning, yippee!

I hear girls shouting, making such a din,
I hope they put their rubbish in the bin.
I see Lily standing at the door,
I don't think she can take anymore,
Is that the bell I hear, I jump for glee,
Thank goodness school is over, it's three.

Kelly-Louise Franks (12)
St Mary's High School

THINGS I LIKE TO DO

I like to watch the
newborn lambs skipping
round the fields
in spring.

I like to go to
the beach or the
swimming pool in
the hot summer.

I like kicking all
the different coloured leaves
round, that coat the
ground in autumn.

I like to catch the dripping
snowflakes on my tongue
when it snows in
the cold winter.

Michelle Rice (12)
St Mary's High School

MY BEAUTY

My heart is deeper than the ocean
And filled with beautiful emotion,
The blood that circles round my heart,
Shall finally run out.
But my love is totally true
And shall always be with you.

I find you very polite,
That's one of the reasons we rarely fight,
Another thing is that you care,
That's how we make a loving pair,
You are also very kind,
That's what makes us bind.

When I kiss your lips, I feel your love,
My mind just flies like a dove,
I look at your eyes and see into them,
I feel like I'm being sucked into your den.
I touch your hair, then I realise,
You're not my duty, but my beauty.

Duana Rooney (14)
St Mary's High School

THOSE CREEPY EYES

Those beady eyes
Staring at me.
Those beady eyes
Is it the TV?

I take a step
My heart trembles with fear.
Bump, bump, bump, bump
As petrified as I am, I freeze on the spot.

Those eyes move about
All over the door frame.
They stare and they blink
Although still fix on me.

I take another step forward.
I hawk my head round,
To see if I dare
Find what's staring at me.

I realise I know those eyes.
I think I find the eyes
Are my mum's but she's at work!
I gulp and have a lump in my throat.

Afraid to cough
I choke on the lump.
There is sweat running down my forehead
For soon I fear I may be dead.

I gulp hard, I have a very dry throat.
I run out of the house like some mad lunatic.
I run to my mum who thinks it fun
But believe me it isn't.

Andrea McGovern (11)
St Mary's High School

ICE CREAM VAN

Being awoken silently by a beam of light
From the sun, which had filtered in
Through a crack in my curtains.

I loved to wake up to the sunny mornings
That the summer had provided.

Summer had always seemed to be made
Perfectly for children.
Long, hot days and cool bright nights.
A sort of treat as you got to eat
Tasty ice cream
And stay out longer at night.

My friends and I on the look out for the
Soothing music of the ice cream van.
The van would make a sudden stop
Each day, to see little boys and girls full of
Delight, pounding on the van, pushing and shoving.
One by one each to be served with an
Ice cream well deserved.

Years went on with fun-filled summers,
Until one day no music to be heard from
The ice cream van,
We waited and waited but still
No ice cream man.

Olivia Powell (14)
St Mary's High School

WITCH, WITCH

Witch, witch, where do you fly,
Over the treetops right into the sky.
Here she goes down by the alley,
Watch out, here comes the wicked witch Annie.
Her black cloak and pointed hat,
Tap, twiddle and zap.
Oh look there goes one, two, three of her weird looking bats.
'I failed to proceed with my horrible deed
But I'll come back soon and this time I will succeed.'

So the wicked witch Annie went back to her den,
To read up on her books and fetch her cat, Ben.
Off they went shooting up across the heavens,
Like stars creeping along in the dark in their sevens.
Then she starts chanting her spell
So that all the wicked witches would rule and leave
                              some mortals to dwell.
But as always she and her gang never succeed
For the good mortals rule
And the wicked witches drool.

Elaine Byrne (13)
St Mary's High School

A HORSE FROM THE BAY

There was a young horse from the bay
Who always enjoyed eating hay
He went to sleep
Beside some sheep
And didn't wake up till the next day.

Amy McDonnell (11)
St Mary's High School

BORING STUFF AT HOME

I hate being stuck inside all the time,
When I could be outside exploring the
Wildlife and nature.
I hate doing homework or helping my mum
Oh just so boring.

Sometimes I wish I lived on my own
And I could do whatever I wanted,
Like going to the woods and playing
Outside in the fresh air.

But that will not happen for a long time,
Only once a week I hear the swish of the
Swallows that make me nice and cold.
But now I have to be stuck inside doing
Boring old homework! Sigh!

Karen Convery (11)
St Mary's High School

HALLOWE'EN

Witches cackling all night long,
Ghosts humming their spooky song.
Children knocking at the doors,
Trick or treating, sweets galore.
Bonfire lighting up the sky,
Bats flying around the sky.
Fireworks banging all night long,
Horror movies on TV
Here's a message from me
'Happy Hallowe'en!'

Sinead McGrath (11)
St Mary's High School

HALLOWE'EN

While ghosts and ghouls fly through the air,
Making little children scared.
Witches and wizards fly on their brooms,
Right across the sunlit noon.

As they fly through the sky,
Cats miaow and wolves they cry.
While witches cast their evil spells,
Dreams fall down the wishing wells.

If you see a blood-thirsty vampire,
Be sure you know to light a fire.
If you see another stranger,
I assure you there will be danger!

So that's the end of Hallowe'en,
I hope your dreams don't make you scream.

Shaunna Ferns (11)
St Mary's High School

WITCHES, VAMPIRES AND GHOSTS

Witches, vampires and ghosts
will be glad to be your hosts.
It's Hallowe'en and it's time to scream.
So join us tonight, to frighten your neighbours
and listen to things that go *bump* in the night.
So grab your black cat, broom and mask
and join us in our task of making
you remember this time with your hosts.
So never forget the *witches, vampires and ghosts.*

Ciara Mooney (11)
St Mary's High School

RELATIONSHIP

Bye Michelle
It's very hard to die
Just think of all those pretty birds in the sky.
That will get your mind off it for a while.

Sit back, take a break
Think of all those lies you told me
And flies you put in my cup of tea.
Have them cos they're no use to me
And *get out!*

See you soon (not)
You stupid silly balloon.
You have just ruined our relationship.
Just think, I was the black sheep of the family.

Natasha McDonald (11)
St Mary's High School

AUTUMN

It's blustery, it's cold, it's raining outside.
The children are all running and trying to hide.
The summer is out, the autumn is here
And then it's Hallowe'en time of the year.

It's then the noise will start to begin.
The bangers will bang,
The fireworks will squeal.
The children will start to trick or treat
And will be scaring people on the streets.

Linda McGarry (12)
St Mary's High School

MY SISTER

My sister to me
seems very tall,
but maybe it's because
I'm so small.

Her shoes won't fit me,
they're far too big.
Her hair is so thick,
it looks like a wig.

We both share a room,
which really is a drag.
When we are arguing
I call her a bag.

She screams at me,
and calls me a midget.
I just say, 'Do you want to be hit?'
This seems to calm her down a bit.

We don't always fight,
we usually agree.
My sister I know
she really loves me.

Sheila Meagher (12)
St Mary's High School

DEATH IN THE CITY

Crash, bang, fireball
Up on the tower tall.

Run, panic, scream
It must be a dream.

Terror came from the sky
New Yorkers cry, 'Why oh why?'

Oh! Here comes another
As a maniac hits the second tower.

Creak and groan and rumble
To the ground the twins did tumble.

Thousands lie buried there
As dark and dust fill the air.

Marie Claire McAteer (14)
St Mary's High School

HALLOWE'EN POEM

Hallowe'en has come again
Children hoping it does not rain.
Fireworks lighting up the sky
As people tuck into apple pie.

Bonfires piled ever so high.
'Oh how dangerous!' the old lady said with a sigh.
Children running to and fro
Shouting to each other where to go.

Fireworks blasting into the night,
Causing people such a fright.
Animals are terrified
Looking for places to hide.

Eventually there is peace at last.
Hallowe'en is in the past.

Aine Larkin (11)
St Mary's High School

NEW YORK

Today we look on
as the buildings are gone.

As the aeroplanes drove on,
the two buildings are gone.

The sorrow in our faces,
the tears that people shed
now that the buildings are gone
many people are dead.

The people in New York,
all stood in shame
as they all looked on
at the buildings they
knew were all gone.

All the emptiness now
inside as they search for
their loved ones
but all they have to do
is just try and try.

Roisin Lennon (14)
St Mary's High School

AMERICA

The 11th of September
I'll never forget
The day that the world
Was in deep shock.
The twin brothers
Were once so tall
But now they lie on
America's floor.

The people we lost
Will never come back
But some still hope.
For beneath the two towers
Are loved ones so near.
We pray for their safety
Their lives are so dear.

Aine McEvoy (13)
St Mary's High School

NEW YORK TROUBLES

On the 11th September 2001,
The fighting in America had just begun.
A terrible trouble,
Burst our bubble.
Because of two aeroplanes,
Things won't be the same again.

Two twin brothers that stood so tall,
But now there's nothing there at all.
At a quarter to nine,
All was fine.
But by eleven,
Many had left for Heaven.
Those buildings so high,
Made so many die.
A terrible crash,
Destroyed New York with a mighty clash.

Many people wait in despair,
In hope to find their loved ones . . .
Somewhere.

Deirbhle O'Brien (13)
St Mary's High School

THE FRIGHT OF THE NIGHT

In the middle of the night,
I reach for the light
And let out a squeal
As something furry I feel.

What is this
That has made my heart miss?
I hear a creak
And let out a squeak.

I want to get out of bed
But I crawl under the quilt instead.
What can it be
That has just scared me?

I risk a look
And reach for a book,
To throw at the mouse
That has just moved into my house.
Out you marauder!
You furry invader!

The mouse turns tail
As I rant and rail.
I know I was scared
At the noises I heard
But the mouse got a fright
And went into the night.

Leaving me to switch off the light.

Clare McShane (12)
St Mary's High School

IN AMERICA

The streets grew quiet.
Fear was upon everyone.
People started to cry, scream, roar.
No one knew whether their
Brothers, sisters, parents
Or any relatives
Were in the tower
When the plane hit.

Everyone was running around
Afraid their own lives would be endangered.

Bang!

The second tower was hit
Everyone went mad.
People were trembling
Holding anyone near.
Screaming for their lives.

While we sat in our
Safe homes
Watching the news
And the only thing
We could do was
Pray!

Adele Sarsfield (13)
St Mary's High School

MY BIRTHDAY

I woke up early one morning,
Just before entering the day,
I planned a day so busy
With my friends I had to play.

You see it was my birthday,
Today I will be eleven,
It seems like only yesterday,
I turned the age of seven.

That was the day I got my puppy,
I never will forget,
Its beautiful, shiny, fluffy coat,
That's why I called him Jet.

As I climb out of bed,
I called his name out loud.
'Where are you Jet?' I said again
But he wasn't to be found.

But then I met my mummy,
She looked really sad,
'Oh Cassie,' she said, 'I'm sorry
It really is quite bad.'

She sat me on her knee,
And told me Jet had died.
I'll never forget my birthday,
Because I cried and cried and cried.

I wake up now each morning,
Just before entering the day
But I pause for just a moment,
And a prayer to Jet I say!

Cassie Kelly (11)
St Mary's High School

SAD

Lying there with my mouth wide open.
Inside I was yelping, screaming and shouting for help
But the man just stood there looking over me by the roadside.
Laughing and laughing at me with the stab wound in my side.
My life was flashing before my eyes.
I wanted to jump up and shout, 'Let me live my life you guys!'
But I knew I was on my last few breaths of air.
I thought of all my precious family and how much I loved them.
Then there were my friends, these great people every one of them.
'Everyone's time has to come!' I said. 'But why so young?'
Then slowly the man walked away as I passed away.
My life shattered.

Marian McConville (13)
St Mary's High School

THE WITCH ANGEL

There once was a witch named Drizzela,
She slept on a golden pillar.
She said it was nice to eat some mice
But children always taste better.

I went down to her house one night
And I saw such a terrible sight.
It gave me a tremendous fright.
No longer a witch
An angel.

Catherine McArdle (11)
St Mary's High School

WAR BEGINS

No one will forget the 11th of September,
It will live on in history forever.
The once proud standing towers of capitalism
Are nothing but a heap of metal and rubble,
Nothing but the skeletal outline remains.

The buildings fell and the dust rose
Turning the bright sky dark
As the heavens at night, dust
Settled and people started searching,
Sirens screamed, people cried,
The mouths of others were dry
As the dust as they gasped the air.

The rest of the country,
The rest of the world
Stood in an eerie silence,
The world was full of tears,
Anger, sorrow and confusion
All at the same time.

Days later emergency workers
Covered in white dust scavenged
Through the rubble like machines
Looking for fallen comrades.
The only thing that sustained them.
Feelings of horror and hope.
In one day, one incident, the hopes
And dreams of America crumpled
Like the towers of capitalism,
Crushed to death in Manhattan.

Sean Trainor (13)
St Paul's High School

WE LIKE NOISE

The ring of a phone, the ding of a bell,
The pitch of a salesman trying to sell.
The clap of a hand, the click of a case,
The spinning of wheels at the start of a race.
The buzz of a bee, the hum of a tune,
The snap and pop of a bursting balloon.
The dummm . . . in a piano, the echo in a shell,
The sobbing of a little boy in a dusty stairwell.
The rush of the wind, the trickle of rain,
The grumble of people in a battered old train.
The boom of a radio, the roar at the bar,
The squeals of a singer, it's rather bizarre.
The whoosh of the wind, the rumble of thunder,
The drone of a man in a drunken blunder.
The slap of a ruler, the crack of a cane,
The scrapping of leaves on an old tattered drain.
The clock of a pen, the vroom of a car,
The drip from the tap on the cold steel bar.
The crack of a rifle, the cheer of a man,
The sizzle of sausages on a very hot pan.
The scrape of the chalk, the slam of a door,
The jeer of a crowd when the opposing team scores.
The clink of the keys, the splash in the pool,
The boy shouting out, acting the fool.
We like noise!

Darren McCann (12)
St Paul's High School

WINTER

Short days,
Grey clouds,
Wet roads,
Stormy seas,
Deep puddles,
Gushing drains,
Frosty fields,
Starry skies,
Snowy hedges,
Winter.
Cold fingers,
Cracked lips,
Scarfed necks,
Blue noses,
Pinched toes,
White faces,
Wrapped babies,
Windswept shoppers,
Hurrying pedestrians,
Courageous cyclists,
Winter.
Warm houses,
Cosy fires,
Hot drinks,
Cooked breakfast,
Savoury mince pies,
Lighting windows,
Decorated trees,
Twinkling lights,
I love winter.

David Hughes (14)
St Paul's High School

GOD BLESS AMERICA

On the 11th of September
The Twin Towers came down.
Many humans died in this atrocity,
Irish, English, Americans too.

The suicide bombers
Had a fanatical faith,
Men on planes took them down.

Innocent people lost their lives,
It was a tragic day,
The sharp smell of kerosene filled the air.

Many survived the crumbling towers
Only to be trapped underground,
The rescue workers couldn't reach them in time,
They died a horrible death.

The people behind this cannot hide.
There must be justice
But no innocent should die.

God will look over this mess and cry
For many people have died.
They are now with God
And they are now truly happy
Way up there in the sky.
Oh why did so many people have to die?

Christopher Cranney (14)
St Paul's High School

SHATTERED

I watched as it happened,
The two towering twins flattened.

When those planes crashed
All the steel and glass was smashed.

Two towers crumbling to the ground,
Symbols of wealth and power profound.
All those people's lives are gone,
Such a sad day for everyone.

Shoulder to shoulder in sorrow,
No one know what's coming tomorrow.

We pray for the relatives of people who died,
They have no place where they can hide
From terror and pain,
Anguish in vain.
We hope for all who are there,
And for world peace everywhere.

Kelly McGuirk (13)
St Paul's High School

TOWERING TRAGEDY

New York, New York,
So good they named it twice.
At 2 o'clock in broad daylight
The Twin Towers were blown out of sight.

I turned on the news and watched in vain,
From my TV I could feel the pain.
A world in shock, a river of tears,
People on board the planes filled with fear.

Families mourning living in hope,
We are praying so they can cope.
11th September 2001
It will be hard to forgive for what has been done.

We pray that war won't break,
Even if it is only for children's sake.
We don't want our dreams to be dashed,
We want a future that won't be smashed.

Orlagh Boyle (13)
St Paul's High School

GRANNY'S HAPPY HOME

Granny's happy home will always
Linger in my mind.

The sweet aroma of her home
Cooking was like a welcoming smile.

Many a happy hour spent playing in
Her king-sized garden.

Hiding in the tall green grass,
Paddling in the glistening stream
Behind the old rustic wooden fence.

Built a tree house from left-over wood
And old patterned carpet,
On the moss covered apple tree that
Stood at the garden side.

Nothing but a pile of rubble now stands
At my granny's happy home.

Lauren O'Grady (14)
St Paul's High School

OUR WHITE PONY

I remember when I was young,
We had a pony called Scruffy.
He was white with a sparkling silver shine,
When we washed him he was all fluffy.

The thing I remember most
Is when he hauled me across the floor
When I forgot to let go of the rope,
As he ran for my brother's apple core.

I also remember
My first trot with him,
When his hair was sleeked with silvery sweat,
Hobbling because of his sore limb.

But unfortunately he was sold
A few years ago,
But I have another pony now,
Another white pony as you now know.

Jennifer Hughes (13)
St Paul's High School

THE TREE IN THE MEADOW

There is a tree in the meadow
That as a child I couldn't climb,
It is an enormous oak tree
That is in the middle of the meadow.

At first I tried to climb the tree
But I couldn't climb this enormous tree.
It was as big as a house
And as enormous as the shops.

When I got older I could climb the tree
That is in the middle of the meadow.
Every day I would go to the tree with my friends,
We played all day long in its arms.

Thomas Casey (14)
St Paul's High School

THE TREE HOUSE AND ITS MAGICAL WONDERS

The filthy, crumbling tree house
Facing my granny's old cottage.
It was not kept very well,
Us coming in dirty, Mummy giving us hell.

Cows meal bags made
Into slides to play.
Messing with my cousins
In the mud and clay.

A big hawthorn tree stood
Beside a ruined ivy wall.
A look-out point
For people who call.

'What do you do up there,'
My granda would say.
'Oh, it's a secret
We must not say.'

And then summer ended
And nights grew colder.
The tree house magic is gone
For another year when we're older.

Feilin Quinn (13)
St Paul's High School

A NIGHT IN A TENT

'Lights out! Lights out!'
My parents shout.
It's scary out here,
There might be an earwig in my ear.
The owl hoots, the trees sway,
There's something out there,
I promise you, I swear.

I hear a crunch, I hear a cry,
What will I do? Will I stay in and hide?
There's a figure outside,
What could it be?
Let me see it's coming closer to me.
Heart thumps harder,
Shivering spine,
What could it do?
Chop this head of mine.

What do you think I did see when I peeped?
But this terrible monster,
Was a huge woolly sheep!

Danielle Lynch (13)
St Paul's High School

THE AMERICAN TRAGEDY

A terrible day,
But the terrorists will pay.

Did it signal the end of the world,
When all those people from on high were hurled?

A great city's hopes were dashed,
As the hatred lashed.

Mighty buildings crumbled,
One hundred stories tumbled.

Fireman, ambulances and police,
Searched hour upon hour without cease.

The whole world prays
For peace in these dramatic days.

Amanda McTaggart (13)
St Paul's High School

OUR SECOND HOME

My friends and I
Had a tree hut
Very high up and dangerous
With furniture and a ladder.

We only knew where it was,
Nobody else knew.
We were always there,
It's like our second home.

We did everything in it,
We played in it,
We ate in it,
And we even fought in it.

People found it,
We had to find a new one
But this time
It was far away.

Vanessa McParland (13)
St Paul's High School

PEACE IN THE WORLD

We want peace,
Peace in the world,
No wars or fights,
Some people want to
Go out at night.

There are days we pray that
Fights and wars will go away.
My parents always said,
Do not disobey.

There are people who have wars
For their countries,
And other people who do
It for someone.

There are people on the run
For doing things they should
Not have done,
If you asked them they would
Say they were doing it for fun.

There are people in prison
For a lot of things,
But we only know the
Half of what they did.

I want to keep away
From them kind of people,
I don't want to get a bad name
I just want everyone to be the same.

We would not like friends
Who would do bad things,
Like selling stolen goods
To make a few quid.

Peace in the world we want,
So come on everyone and pray.

Gavin Magee (14)
St Paul's High School

THE TRAUMATIC TUESDAY TERROR

A very normal day,
People heading to work
Without delay,
But this was no normal day,
This was the day
America lost heart
And confidence
As they lost two great
Symbols of power,
The World Trade Center
And The Pentagon.

Hundreds of people dying,
Jumping from windows
As if they were birds
Flying from the sky.

As buildings collapsed
Into pulverised dust and rubble
Flames gushed through,
Smoke was rising
And people were dying.

Clare McCann (14)
St Paul's High School

THE OLD, OLD HOUSE

When I was young there was an old house
Where my friends and I would play.
Destroyed as it was, it's where we played,
We loved the old, old house.

We played on the broken-down stairs,
We played on the rotten, wooden beams
That had fallen to the ground.
We played anywhere and everywhere,
We loved the old, old house.

Then when we were nine
A rotten old man went and bought it.
He knocked it down as if it were Lego,
We will miss the old, old house.

Kevin McQuade (13)
St Paul's High School

THE TUNNEL CHILDREN

I remember the old bridge
That we used to hide under,
It was derelict. it was metal,
Brown rusted and beside it
The largest tunnel in the British Isles.
Many a day we walked it,
Hiding from each other
In the little caves in the walls.
It once carried steam trains,
The tracks and sleepers were gone then.
There were only stalagmites and stalactites,
And some bats there then.

Stephen O'Brien (14)
St Paul's High School

MY SUMMERTIME PLAY PLACE

That was our favourite little spot.
That's where we stayed a lot.
That's where we spent our hot summer days.
We loved that place in many ways.
The long grassy grazing field which led to it.
By the rushing river on the large mossy stone we would sit.
We made a tyre swing on one of the many large fingery
Branches of the old oak tree.
When you were on the tyre swing a lovely view you would see,
Large sheep, mountains, leafy tall trees, the lot.
No wonder it was our favourite little spot.

Where? The river of course.

Louise Mullan (14)
St Paul's High School

AMERICA'S TRAGEDY

Oh how could this tragedy happen?
It was nothing but a shock to us all.
Countless lives were taken
As both buildings were demolished.

Oh how my body trembled to watch it,
To think people could plan this and do it all.

Oh how sad my heart is to think that people believe
There is a need to do this and call it their creed.

Paula Keenan (13)
St Paul's High School

ROAD MONSTER

On our own,
Out on the bikes,
Brother, friend and I,
Too young to stay on our own.

Darkness fell
As we climbed the hill but
Going back was a different story.

Bridge of trees,
Brother ahead of me,
Strong wind,
Line of traffic,
Lorry first in line,
Panic, like wind in my head.

Up on the grass,
Bump, bump along
On the asphalt surface,
Down like a bag of cement
Beneath the bike,
Sprawled dizzy on the main road.

Turned to see flashing lights,
Horror held my breath,
Lifted my bike,
Weakened with fright,
First meeting with a road monster.

Eimear Bagnall (13)
St Paul's High School

GROWING UP

I remember when I was young
I was always having fun,
Straight out the old brown door
Shouting to the day in front of me
With an enthusiastic roar.

I remember hearing when I was young,
'Not out of the gate,' from my mum.
Then my friends would come to me
And we'd play in happy company.

I remember when I got older
I was allowed to wander beyond
The big old gate
To run and explore with my mates.
'Stay in the street,' shouted Mum.

I remember when I was eight
I was allowed out of the street,
But where could we go? Only to the shop.
'Wait for the traffic to stop!' was Mum's cry then.

I remember four years ago
I was finally free to go anywhere,
Mostly into town.
Mum would only say, 'Here's a couple of pounds.'

Ciara Grant (14)
St Paul's High School

THE ALL IRELAND CHAMPIONSHIP

On arrival nerves became tense,
as the crowd gathered in one
hall the music played the reel
and a jig as a warming applause.
When I entered the stage the
music began and played beat
after beat as all eyes were set
on watching my feet.

I did my first move and soon
got into the groove. I did my
best and hoped the rest would
come true. I wouldn't have long
to wait now.

The music came to an end as I
bowed and walked proudly off
the stage. There was an out-
standing number of well dones
given to me and I replied, 'It's
good fun dancing up there.'

It came to results as I stood
tensely with number 13, she the
adjudicator said, 'Well done and
1st place goes to number 13.'
My heart was pumping with
joy and so I got up there to
received my prize whilst all I
could hear was my heart
beating in rhyme with the music.

The crowd cheered and cheered
for me to dance once again
and so I did with dignity and
pride in what I had achieved.
At least now I can leave with a
smile on my face, now I am the
champion of 2001.

Michelle Cunningham (13)
St Paul's High School

BLAMED!

Why me?
Everywhere I go, 'It's you!'
I get blamed
Here, there, everywhere.
Guess what?
My brother dropped a
Glass and broke it,
My mum came rushing in
To see what had happened,
Of course, who do you think
Got the blame?
Of course, me!
Oh boy, why me?
Plus my cousin hit
My brother on the head . . .
Yes, me.
'Go to your room.'
Why me?

Charlene Carlon (13)
St Paul's High School

My Granny's Death

The day she retired,
What life was like,
How sad we felt
The day we found her
Candle was out.

We sat beside her bedside,
Our hearts were crushed and sore,
We did our duties till the end,
Till we could do no more.

In tears we watch her sinking,
We watch her fade away,
We will never forget you,
Till we meet again.

Our happiness was taken away
From the day she left us.
Our hearts are fulfilled
With memories we remember
Of what we did each day.

I miss your smile, your joking ways,
I miss the things you used to say,
And when the old times I do recall
It's then I miss you most of all.

From that day on
I'll never forget
For the rest of my life
How I felt
When my granny went.

Catherine Hollywood (13)
St Paul's High School

OUR HUT IN THE FIELD

We used to walk across the fields,
Jump across the river,
My friends and I had so much fun,
Away from everyone.

We found barrels to sit on
Beside the flowing river,
We went there nearly every day
And we built a new hut.

The trees around the fields
Were tall with birds nests,
We sat beside the river
And had a lot of fun.

The grass was long
And tickled our legs,
The spiders were crawling
Up our arms.

The field was big
With lots of trees,
And had long grass to play in.

We had a good time there,
Had so much fun together.
My friends and I
We're never shy
When we were together.

Sharon Toal (13)
St Paul's High School

OUT OF IRELAND AND INTO AMERICA

Out of Ireland of the green, grassy fields.
Out of Ireland of the windy seas.
Out of Ireland of the poitin still.
Out of Ireland of the dairy cows.
Out of Ireland of the emerald valleys.

Into England of the powerful government.
Into England of the emigrating slaves.
Into England of the aroma of tea.
Into England of the rich and arrogant landlords.
Into England of the dominating town people.

Into America of the powerful white people.
Into America of the abolished slaves.
Into America of the dusty gravel roads.
Into America of the cotton picking plantation.
Into America, the home of emigrant hope.

Padraig Rogers (13)
St Paul's High School

MY FRIEND

Straight from the heart
This is coming your way,
You're a friend to me,
You help me through the day,
We work, we play, we talk on the phone,
With you as a friend I'll never be alone.

Sarah McIntyre (13)
St Paul's High School

SUMMER IN THE WOODS

The grassy bank shadows the glistening water
While the sun beats off my face.
Sound trapped by a canopy of silence,
Not a voice, not a bark,
Truly a beautiful place.

Only the trees speak
With their glamorous leaves
Dancing in a cascade of sunbeams,
While the river trickles down the jagged
Edge plummeting to Earth.
Memories of this place
Will always linger on
Of how I walked in the woods.

Caolan McKeown (14)
St Paul's High School

AMERICA AT ITS CORE

Tragedy struck,
The life and soul of New York City
Crumbled to dust in an avalanche of debris,
To a terrible chorus of cries.

As people mourned the dead,
Rescue workers began the search
Among the mountains of rubble.
And still, they search to find hope
And life amid the heaving heart
Of central Manhattan.

Danielle Brady (13)
St Paul's High School

SPOOKY POEM

One dark night, I went into my room
And what did I see? Only a witch on a broom.
I looked out the window,
And what did I see?
Only her cat's beady eyes looking back at me.

I went out to the hall and what did I see?
Only a big black spider
Right in front of me.

I went down the creaky stairs
And out through the door,
And what did I see?
A gruesome zombie on the floor.

I ran down the road
And turned to the right,
And a werewolf jumped out
And gave me a fright.

All of a sudden
The lights started to flash,
And what did I hear?
Only wallop, bang, crash.

I started to run home
Hoping nothing was there,
But what stood in the doorway
Was a big hairy bear.

I threw a stone at the bear
But it bounced off and broke,
And all of a sudden
I awoke.

Denise Leonard (12)
St Paul's High School

PEACE

Green and orange come together,
Break down the barricades,
Stop the senseless,
Drop the guns,
End the ignorance,
Discuss the differences,
Don't fight them.

How many must die?
How many lives ruined?
Couples torn apart,
Parents with dead kids,
Children orphaned,
How long till this stops?

All for what?
RC or P written on papers,
What school we attend,
Where we go on Sundays, Church or Mass,
Where we shop or live.

If this were to stop
We would find friends beyond religion,
Lives would be saved,
Friends would be made.

Terrorists who have ruled our lives for so
Long will have to be beaten.
We'll have ended their control of our lives.
We can live free from harassment and
Threats from bigots.

Declan Byrne (13)
St Paul's High School

COLOURS

Colours mean a lot to me,
Not just in my clothes,
It covers many ways of life
With friends and with foes
From north and south
And east and west,
The seasons come and go.

Planes and trains are full of colour
Going from place to place,
A smile, a wave, white, black,
A scene in every face.
Colours from this life we have
From deep within our minds.

We still got the darkest colours
When the bright ones refuse to shine.
They can also form our moods,
Lift us up or leave us behind,
Amaze us with the roaring seas
And confuse us with the blind.

Colours form our love,
Donations red and kind.
Colours form our hatred,
Dark red and grey combined.
All we have is one chance
To stand up and to shine.
I prefer the truest colours
But some truths are hard to find.

Eva Woods (15)
St Paul's High School

MY LITTLE FIELD HUT

It lies in a hollow in the long grassy field,
Near a stream that trickles in the winter.
A gate separates it from the land,
A wooden stool connected to a bare bush.

It is cosy and it is covered in branches,
Animals of some sort always there,
Making their screeching, snorting sounds
As the birds twitter in the trees.

Many strange scents and odours
Drift upon the silent air.
The slurry, the wildlife,
The trees and the flowers mixed scent.

We'd sit and play for hours
Around the back of my home,
Until the farmer drove by our hollow
Bumping big in the seat of his tractor.

We'd take a leap off the gate,
Over the bank and away round the estate.
The farmer out of sight
We returned to our favourite spot.

Our little field hut
Around the back of my home.

Jennifer Smyth (13)
St Paul's High School

OUT OF IRELAND

Out of Ireland, wrecked with famine,
Out of Ireland, poverty all around,
Out of Ireland, where starvation cuts through,
Out of Ireland, what will we do?

Into England, no famine there,
Into England, people flee Ireland,
Into England, where there's food and land,
Into England, where there is freedom in the air.

Into America, this is the New World,
Into America, hear the Yanks talk,
Into America, a long journey worthwhile,
Into America, we found our home at last.

Noleen Carragher (14)
St Paul's High School

MAISY

I know a woman called Maisy,
Sure everyone thinks she's crazy.
She wears her shoes on the opposite feet
And falls asleep sometimes out in the street.
She puts on her clothes inside out
And brushes her hair with a fork.
Sure it's the beer that makes her act so queer,
She's not really crazy, she's just daft.

Christopher Fearon (13)
St Paul's High School

A FRIEND

A friend to me, I wish you'd be,
Forever and a day,
With thoughts of love, care and sharing
We'll take along the way.

Responding to our every need,
With friendship by our side,
Knowing our deepest thoughts,
Our feelings deep inside.

Compassion is the strongest gift
In you I always see,
Like the sunrise in the morning
You brightly shine for me.

Knowing in my deepest heart
Your heart from deep inside,
We share our inner secrets
And cherish them with pride.

I know some day in death we'll part,
I never will surrender,
I'll be with you in paradise,
But friends, we'll be forever!

Lisa Daly (13)
St Paul's High School

JUST ANOTHER TUESDAY?

It was just another Tuesday,
Or was there something else?
People going to work,
Children going to school,
Some catching buses,
Others in traffic jams.

People boarding planes,
Dreaming of happiness in new places.
Little did they know
This would be their last journey.
These planes were hi-jacked
And were flown into the Twin Towers
Killing thousands of people,
Screams were heard.
People jumping out of buildings.
Rescuers crushed by rubble.
People's lives destroyed in a matter of minutes.
All this tragedy. But why?
September 11th the darkest day.

Lisa Fitzgerald (14)
Sacred Heart Grammar School

LEFT BEHIND

Why didn't he collect me,
At twenty-five past three?
Something must have happened.
What's it going to be?

I hope it's not my mum,
I hope it's not my dad.
What if someone's hurt?
What if it makes me sad?

Maybe it isn't serious
I might be making a fuss.
Oh no! I just remembered,
I was meant to get the bus!

Rebecca O'Hare (13)
Sacred Heart Grammar School

LET ME GO!

All they ever say is *'No!'*

'Mum, can I go to the cinema?'
'No! Sally, I told you last night you're not allowed to go!'
'But Mum, everyone is going.'
'I don't care if the Pope is going, you're not going,'

All they ever say is *'No!'*

It's not fair
None of my parents care!
I just want to have a bit of fun,
But in their eyes eating a bun is even fun.
They're just too old,
They even tell me I'm bold.

All they ever say is *'No!'*

I wish I was older,
They'd probably say I was even bolder.
I would love to be a pop star.
I could even go and have a drink in the bar.
They'd say 'You're still too young.'
I don't even get a say,
It's just not fair.

All they ever say is *'No!'*

Sarah Jane Quinn (13)
Sacred Heart Grammar School

SWALLOWS

Swallows soar high in the sky
Letting nothing pass their way.
Gliding with strong winds,
Swooping through the cool air.

When autumn winds rush in,
The swallows know, it's time to go
To the warm soft airs of Africa.

Our winter is long and cold.
The woods are silent as we await,
The swallows to come back.

One morning in May I hear a happy song
Telling us the winter is over.
Small grey shapes arrive from the distance.
They circle the roof tops
Looking for new homes.
They nest in ivy chains,
Or dark sooty chimneys,
Feeding their young with little insects.

Marguerite Sherry (11)
Sacred Heart Grammar School

RYAN GIGGS

The world's greatest player,
There is no doubt,
The best midfielder
You've seen about.

He's got pace,
He's got skill
And a run
That could kill.

He plays for Man United
The best team in the land,
And for Wales he wears
The captain's armband.

His name is Ryan,
He's a lovely man,
Better than
Beckham, Butt, Cole and Stam.

Deirdre Rocks (12)
Sacred Heart Grammar School

LUCKY

I love my dog Lucky
He is cuddly and fluffy
If I am feeling down
He is always there.

I love my dog Lucky
I play with him every day
As soon as I get home from school
He's waiting at the door.

I love my dog Lucky
He loves going on walks and
When he sees his lead he runs around
In circles, like a washing machine.

I love my dog Lucky
I wonder every day
What I would do
If Lucky ran away!

Aoife Treanor (12)
Sacred Heart Grammar School

THE IMP

The evening shadows, short and dark,
On the ground they leave no mark.
As daytime's noise and bustle cease,
A blanket of tiredness starts to creep
Up across my leg and torso too
And colours my eyes with shades of blue.
My soul floats high, lighter than air,
Looks down on my body lying motionless there.

A light beneath my bed I see,
Creeps slowly like the roots of a tree.
Across the mat, towards the door,
A small figure scurries across the floor,
Into my cupboard he throws out my clothes,
He knocks over my books that were set out in rows.
He breathes on my window and draws silly signs,
Then swings on my curtains and creases my blinds.

He flies round my face with wings like a bat,
And stares out my window with eyes like a cat.
He spits on my mirror with a tongue like a newt,
Tips over my talcum and leaves prints of his boot.
He stands on his three legs and surveys the scene,
I rub my eyes thinking 'This must be a dream!'
Then with an evil smile on his face
He slithers back into his dark place.

My mum comes in, in the morning light,
She shakes my shoulder, I jump with fright.
'You should be ashamed of this mess,' she said.
'It wasn't me, it was the imp beneath my bed.'

Cristin Ruddy (13)
Sacred Heart Grammar School

The Early Morning Call!

When I'm snuggled up in bed
Lovely dreams inside my head
Warm and cosy here I'll stay
Sleeping and snoring all the day
What's that awful noise I hear?
It's the alarm clock that I fear.
Now my mum will rant and rave
Dad's in the bathroom having a shave.
Time to get up, sister wails
Brother moans, he never fails.
Mum's on the rampage, hear her shout
I'll have to get up now, there's no doubt.
'Five more minutes, Mum,' I plead
'I won't be late, I'll wash with speed.'
'Down the stairs now, Miss, this minute,'
'Oh keep your hair on, let me finish.'
'Clean your teeth, the breakfast's ready.'
Down the stairs now, stumbling, not steady,
'Morning Mum,' I quickly mumble
As over the dog I fall and stumble,
Pull my socks up, straighten my tie
Down the garden path I fly,
Eating toast and brushing my hair
Half-past eight and I don't care.
Dad's in the car with a face like thunder,
Late again and it's no wonder.
Off to school, we're on our way
To begin another day.

Marianna McParland (13)
Sacred Heart Grammar School

DAD

When Mum says no I get sad
And then I get a thought and
all of a sudden it's 'Oh Dad.'
When my annoying brothers
leave me in pain,
I just shout 'Dad'
and they get the blame.
If I'm going into town
and have no money to spend
I nicely ask Dad who
has money to lend.
If I want something
that Mum can't buy,
I go off to Dad,
pretend to sulk or cry.
There are lots of things I do
which I can't tell
but I get away with it
all because I'm Dad's
Little angel.

Helen McAteer (13)
Sacred Heart Grammar School

MY LITTLE SISTER

A soft, smooth flowing waterfall,
A small, strong willow,
An ever-growing snowball,
Collecting all there is to know.

Her eyes are a deep river that flows,
Her hair is the sky, silky smooth and sleek,
Her cheeks are a dark red rose,
This little life is never bleak.

In-between the ravens is a dove,
A sea horse in the sea,
The little baby we all love,
Yeah! Her name's Cathy.

Kellie Rogers (12)
Sacred Heart Grammar School

THE WALK

I walked out the door
Listening to all the talking
Why is she going out so late?
No more listening, just walking.

As I walked down our street
I felt happy and glad
Then I thought about my family
It made me feel rather sad.

I'm not really walking,
I'm running away
The problem is no one asked me to stay
Any other family would be feeling hurt or pain
Not my family, they're probably worried about bad weather or rain.

I decided to go home to show I cared
But really I'm going home because I'm scared
I thought I was coming home to a normal house
But everything was as quiet as a mouse.

Everyone has been going insane
She could have been beaten up
That's all I could hear
I'll never run away again.

Nicole Curran (12)
Sacred Heart Grammar School

FORGOTTEN OLD TOYS

When you go to the shops or parks
Many children surround you,
Either bawling and yelling in Marks & Sparks
Or being wheeled along with the flu.

But every screaming kid
Has one thing in common,
A fluffy toy for the favourite son
Or a Jack-in-the-box with a lid.

When these kids grow older
They leave their toys behind,
All shoved into a box shoulder to shoulder,
The sad thing is the toys don't seem to mind.

But in the hearts of those lonely dolls
All they want to do is play,
But no one hears their little calls
That fill the house all day.

So if you happen to be reading this
And staring at an abandoned toy
Walk over and give it a kiss,
It's fine if you're a boy.

For long ago that little toy
Was all your pride and joy.

Rosanna Moore (12)
Sacred Heart Grammar School

NICKELODEON

Sister Sister is the show
With Tia and Tamara,
`Go twins go!
Lisa designs dresses galore
And Ray is the one who is a bit of a bore.

Sabrina is a teenage witch,
With magic flowing from her fingertips,
Salem's the cat
Two wacky aunts complete the trio,
Fun and adventure, you get the picture.

Mary Kate and Ashley,
The cool Olsen twins,
Little grown-ups who know it all,
Just turned thirteen, but going on twenty,
Their professor dad has troubles plenty.

Moesha is a teenage girl,
Hanging with friends in her local cafe.
Her dreadlocks are a big attraction,
But she's really quite sweet and full of action.

Now you know how I spend my time,
Television programmes are just divine.
Too much TV I know is bad,
But that's my life, oh dear, how sad.

Megan Duffy (12)
Sacred Heart Grammar School

LOVE AND PAIN, IS IT ALWAYS THE SAME?

Sometimes goodbyes are not forever
And I always see us together.
Holding hands and never letting go,
Some way we're gonna' make them know
Just the way we feel about each other.
Don't worry baby, you'll always be my lover.

You always said you loved me
And you'd never let me go.
We always held our heads up high
And never hung them low.
The love I have for you
Will never go away.
I love you more and more
With every passing day.

As we went out separate ways
I knew we'd meet again.
I knew this thing would never last,
The thing that we call pain!

Tina Greenan (12)
Sacred Heart Grammar School

JAPANESE BLOOD GRASS

Golden light illuminates
The Japanese blood grass
Red intensified in the dew,
Swaying in the wind as time blows past.

Tips covered with blood,
Rivers of mortality, life, energy, love.
Time now to flow into the earth,
Slipping into winter's glove.

Ever precious, insignificant as the gentle wind
Re-emerging, the life cycle rolls on,
Carrying the code, ancestor's blood
From Nippon.

Aisling Hollowood (13)
Sacred Heart Grammar School

QUESTIONS

How did it start? What?
The Earth, how did it begin?
Did God send angels down to plant seeds,
Or did the Earth just transform?
Where did we come from?
Where did school come from?

Why do I have to get up at 7:30?
Why do we have to spend seven hours in school?
Why do we have to do homework?
Is seven hours in school not enough?
And why can't we have computers instead of pens?
Why do teachers make us work?

What is for dinner?
Why can't I go out to play?
Can we go to Jamaica for Christmas?
Why can't I shave my brother's head or why not mine?
Why do I have to go to bed at the same time as him?
Why do we have to eat a balanced diet?

Why are there so many questions
For adults and children to answer and ask?
Why? Why? Why?

Sinead Gorman (12)
Sacred Heart Grammar School

JEWEL!

Jewel's the name of my dog,
She loves to chew on a log,
She likes the other dogs,
And once chased a frog.

She lies in the sun,
Then gets up for a run,
It's a pity she can't drink rum,
'Cause Jewel's loads of fun.

We couldn't pick a name,
Oh! The shame,
It's my brother I blame.
She's got loads of spots
And little dots.
She's a dog with loads of patience
'Cause she's a Dalmatian!

Aisling Walls (12)
Sacred Heart Grammar School

WINTER

A cold winter night
A snowy owl hoots
As it eats its prey.

The air is cool,
There is no one around.
Darkness is close.

Margaret Linsey Murray (12)
Sacred Heart Grammar School

THE HAUNTED HOUSE

On a dark and stormy night
All the children watched in fright.
The house upon the hill up there
Is looking back with such a stare.
The house began to shake and slide
As if to warn them they must hide.
For the master of this house
Isn't a snake nor a mouse,
He is as big as big can be,
And he won't stop not even for me.
He has killed once before
And now he is coming back for more!

Ciara Ryan (12)
Sacred Heart Grammar School

WILLOWS

The willows are long and bendy,
When the wind blows softly
Their leaves swish like water
Dripping over rocks.

As the sun shines brightly
Little birds will sing on the branches,
That sway under their weight.

In storms when the wind howls
Leaves seem to whisper to each other
While flicking and twirling.

Catherine Sherry (11)
Sacred Heart Grammar School

THAT THING!

By the light of the moon,
It was plain to see
Something was lurking by the old oak tree.

What was the thing
That made the cry
And made the shadows pass by?

From near and far
The travellers arrived,
They were lucky enough to have survived.

They went to their homes
Full of wonder,
What was that thing they had seen in the thunder?

They went again
To see the creature
With the devilish eyes and the green skin feature.

Everyone was afraid
That their lives might be in danger,
Was this thing magic, or was it a stranger?

The people were afraid,
They fled the place,
Fear was written all over their face.

Is it a wizard,
Or is it a ghost so white?
Whatever it is it will cause fright!

I remember now,
What my grandad used to say,
Beware of the goblin every single day!

Jennifer Smith (13)
Sacred Heart Grammar School

FRIENDS

Life is too short to lie low
Rise to the highest and let all worries go.
Let them fade into the night sky
So in the morning no one will raise an unwanted eye.

Be still my friend around me,
they'll not get in the way
of the love we have for each other
and the love we bring each day.

Don't let these problems come between us
they are only in harm's way.
My heart cannot control the pain
if anyone should stray.

Everyone can hurt sometimes
But you are not alone.
When you are breaking deep inside
You, my friend, don't have to hide.

I will always be there for you,
especially when you are feeling blue.
So however far or near you are
be it alive or dead.

Our hearts will always hold a bond
that fire and stone can't bend.
So just remember that every day,
our love will never sever away.

Karen Doran (12)
Sacred Heart Grammar School

PLEASE DON'T CRY

Above is a flower, sent to grant a wish,
To erase all those times that have been tough,
Forget about those things in the past,
Time has flown; life's extremely fast.

For all those reasons and many, many more,
Forget those bad times; that broken door.
Those things that were broken are not in the way,
Of life's strange occurrences, this is what I've to say . . .

. . . This one flower alone could put a smile on a face,
And let you get back to guarding your base,
For on the outside; this flower is just a flower;
But in your heart could be so much more.

 Yes, there'll be times you'll want to curl up and die,
Don't worry, there's no need to cry.
Where there are children like us, with love so true,
Who'll be there till the end; yes right through.

We'll give you no reason to want to cry
I hope you'll smile now instead of your sigh.
We'll put no tear upon your face
'Cause we know well, you're truly ace!

Judy Black (13)
Sacred Heart Grammar School

MY WORLD

Step into my world and what do you see?
You'll see my family, friends and then you'll see me.
You'll see the good and bad
You'll see the times when I was lonely, scared and mad.
You'll see how my family fell apart
And all the things I didn't tell you that scarred my heart.

You'll see me when I'm happy, young and carefree
You'll see the memories and how it's good being me.
I only ask of you one thing when you walk out of my world,
That you remember this, the real me
And everything I keep inside of me.

Rosaleen McConville (14)
Sacred Heart Grammar School

MY WORKING DOGS

I have two English springers,
Spaniels, you know.
Used for only shooting over
And not for them nancy shows!

To watch the dogs working
As they hunt through the ditches.
Searching every piece of ground,
Dusty and Gyp, two cracking little bitches.

Both are fully trained
And working on the whistle.
I keep my eyes upon them,
As they drive through some thistle.

Suddenly with a crackle,
A pheasant rockets from the thistle,
My father shoots and shoots again
As I sit the dogs with a whistle.

'Dusty, fetch that's a girl!'
She knows just where to go.
This is what a springer is for,
To hunt and retrieve and not for show.

Joanne Reid (12)
Sacred Heart Grammar School

My Cosy Little Bed

My cosy little bed
Is where I love to be,
Tucked up tight
On a cold and frosty night
Is where I love to be!

When I come home from school each day
I want to rest my weary head
On the soft fluffy pillows that are upon
My cosy little bed!

Every night I climb right in
And curl up in a ball,
I wish for a soft little dream
That will stay with me until dawn.

My cosy little bed
Is where I really love to be,
Especially when it's Saturday
And there's *no school for me!*

Anne Gallagher (12)
Sacred Heart Grammar School

Flowing Water

Flowing water is soothing and gentle,
Flowing down the steep mountain side,
Trickling, tumbling any way it can go,
Falling into the wide open sea,
Or the deep, calm lake.

Ciara McShane (11)
Sacred Heart Grammar School

THE CHILD

Little child, why do you weep?
Sitting in the corner of this narrow street.
Men and women passing by,
noticing you out of the corner of their eye.
They pass you by without a care at all
of this young child sitting by the wall.
You approach them and they begin to retreat,
your stomach rumbles for something to eat.
What's this I see? A coin on the ground,
Too late, down the drain, it's long gone now.
I see his face and I begin to cry.
Why does this child have to suffer and die?
And all those people with loads of money,
couldn't even spare change for his poor family.
And there he lies, no shoes on his feet,
he died of the cold and no food to eat.

Eve Mallon (9)
Sacred Heart Grammar School

KITTENS

Kittens playing in the sun,
All are having tremendous fun.
Cute blue eyes
Trying to catch flies.
Chasing tails,
Swinging from rails.
Cuddling on my knee,
Then scampering free.

Sorcha McCaughley (11)
Sacred Heart Grammar School

CHRISTMAS TIME

As I walk around in the freezing cold
Breathing out small clouds of white, foggy air
I hear bells jingle on trees
And a large, cuddly-looking Santa sitting in a chair.

I observe each small, innocent child,
Jump upon his lap
As excitement fills their faces with glee
And they laugh at his funny, red cap.

As my mind begins to wander
I think of many things
But especially about how I love Christmas
And all the cheer it brings.

Lisa Kelly (13)
Sacred Heart Grammar School

THE SEARCH

They come at night,
And search before sunlight.
They fly around your house on brooms,
To see what they can see in your room.

With their pointed hats and long black clothes,
Covering them from head to toe.
Their only friend is their hairy cat,
As they look for children to turn into bats.

If you are lucky, you'll hear them cackle
As they travel past to see what they can tackle.
Some poor boy or even a girl,
Will land in the cauldron for the nightly stir.

Chantal Parsons (12)
Sacred Heart Grammar School

HALLOWE'EN

I lie awake on Hallowe'en night
I hear a banger, what a fright!

I remember when I was younger
I trick or treated to stop my hunger.

Some people can be really stingy
When they give me 5ps I get cringey.

I used to dream about having
a broomstick
My sister says I'm really thick!

My sister says my friends look
good and bad
But she says that I look sad!

Ann Jennings (14)
Sacred Heart Grammar School

QUESTIONS?

Why is the world round?
Why is the grass green?
Why is the sky blue?
Why?
What did God make it for?
What was his mission?
What were his reasons?
What?
These are some questions,
We often want to know.
But some things are better left,
Where God can only go.

Siamsa McDonald (13)
Sacred Heart Grammar School

CHILLING ENIGMA

A subtle whisper
Runs through the trees
Mottled orange and brown
Warning of something more to come
Before the autumn dawn.

The cattle stamp in the byre
Sensing someone near
Yet no one comes, no one calls
Silence is all they hear.

Icy mist covers the land
Flower and animal entwined
Yet through its haunting silver veil
A sinister figure lurks behind.

Shadows are banished,
Darkness fades
With sunlight's golden touch.

But its shimmering beams
Cast their glow
Onto a land changed much.

Where silver crystals
Reflecting light
Tell of the enchantment
That took place that night.

When Jack Frost roamed,
His translucent fingers placed
Over spiders' webs
His pattern traced.

Niamh McCaughey (13)
Sacred Heart Grammar School

Oops!

Sitting in the dentist's, waiting,
Niamh and Cathy side by side,
Waiting for a boring check-up,
Slowly, slowly, time they bide.

Cathy starts to yawn and sigh,
While Niamh just sits and stares.
So Cath drones on about her Paul,
And exactly what he wears.

Then Niamh butts in,
'Oh yeah, your Paul,
He really likes Louise.
He couldn't keep his eyes off her
That day we went to Lee's.'

'Oops, I forgot,' giggles Niamh,
'You didn't come that day,
He asked her on a date,
But he told us not to say.'

Meanwhile Cathy's gone all green, you see,
'Cause she's been drinking Coke.
She aims for Niamh and opens up,
So that she can boke!

Niamh gets it all, on her new jeans,
Cathy, smiling happy,
'Silly me!' Cathy whispers.
While Niamh looks kind of scrappy!

Ruth Quinn (12)
Sacred Heart Grammar School

SPOTTED

At evening fall I spot him, his eyes, like frightened beads,
Pecking a potato, a rook among the reeds.

The sun sets on his mantle, no longer black it seems,
But a marbled, mottled medley, transformed by magic beams.

With crooked fingers he reaches out his shifting prey to still,
And with dogged determination, he stabs it with his bill.

Me thinks he is a loner, a gaunt and feeble frame,
When a choir of raucous chanters pours forth and calls his name.

Abandoning his booty, he soars into the sky,
And squinting towards the heavens, I observe the reason why . . .

A chain of beaded ebony, perched high upon the wire,
Assembled for evening vespers, ere they scatter and retire.

Envy stirs within me, at their swooping, swirling grace,
Grinning down from ivory towers at the grounded human race.

And do they ever think about, the frontiers that they cross?
Or is it only people who know borders, who trespass?

Jane Rooney (13)
Sacred Heart Grammar School

JACK FROST

He creeps along the grass,
And across the windowpanes.
He covers up the paths,
And tiptoes down the lanes.

You never see him coming,
He never makes a sound.
But all of a sudden there he is,
Spreading along the ground.

He stops the flowing rivers.
He make the trees stand still.
And if he's never made you shiver,
Then very soon he will.

And then he starts to turn away,
As if he won't be back.
But he will return another day,
This frost who's known as 'Jack'.

Bronagh McNally (14)
Sacred Heart Grammar School

IF ONLY . . .

If only I was beautiful
Tall and thin with wonderful hair
If only I could have self confidence
Be able to walk down the street without a care.

If only there was no school
Then we could do what we wanted all of the time.
If only people weren't so money obsessed
And didn't care about penny, franc or dime.

If only I could own my own horse,
Then fulfilled is what I truly would be,
Then I could win all the showjumping competitions
And then the person on the front of Pony Magazine could be me.

If only we could love and be loved,
And let our feelings and emotions be free,
If only there was world peace
We could all be truly happy.

Emer McGowan (13)
Sacred Heart Grammar School

THE LITTLE YELLOW GLOW

I woke up this morning
The smell of food in the air
I looked around my house, no one was there,
I peeped around the corner, the aroma getting stronger,

I looked in the bedrooms
I searched high and low
To try and find my family
Where in the world did they go?

I heard a yelp of laughter
A friendly face to be found
I reached a little yellow glow in the distance
and a little sound.

I tiptoed down the hall
The kitchen door was closed,
I was to find that, that little yellow glow and sound
was my family searching for me high and low.

I didn't just smell the aroma or tiptoed around,
I tasted what I was to find at that little yellow glow
and little sound.

Cara McCullough (13)
Sacred Heart Grammar School

THE TWIN TOWERS

The planes swooped out of the air so fast
It made one gasp.
In the towers thousands were killed
But others lived.
I will not forget the day
When the twin towers just crumbled away.

Tons of rubble have been lifted away
Some people weep, some people pray.
For their loved ones who are no more
We don't know what the terrorists did this for.
But all we know is that the world will always remember
When the thousands died on the 11th of September.

Teresa McCabe (12)
Sacred Heart Grammar School

FRIENDS

Friends are there for you every day of the week,
To sit and listen and let you speak,
To help you through all your troubles,
And help with homework for all those doubles.

Having fun with loud laughter,
No peace to read another chapter,
Going to cinemas, discos or houses,
Just to see those really cool trousers.

Having friends is a part of your life,
Can't wait for your next party night.
In a couple of years you'll still be together,
Laughing and joking, forever and ever.

Party nights are great,
If you are there with a mate,
So don't fall out,
'Cause you need them about.

Through hard and sad times,
Through great and happy times,
They sit and listen and let you speak,
Every day of every week.

Keri Fitzpatrick (13)
Sacred Heart Grammar School

HOMELESS

He sits amid the rubbish bins
In a cold damp doorway on a winter's night,
Begging for coppers and scraps of food
In his tattered old coat. What a pitiful sight.

His face is grimy, his eyes, oh so sad.
His hands cling tightly to his precious sack
Filled with nick-nacks and memories of home,
Of the life he once had. He will never go back.

Afraid to look at the homeless old man,
They all rush past in the pouring rain.
The ragged old man with the shining eyes
His desperate croaks are all in vain.

He's all alone in this cruel big world
Nobody to turn to when he needs some love
No one to be there, just to be there
Nothing but the rain, the moon and the stars above.

He used to dream of a happy life,
Of a friend, his family: the people he'd loved.
And he'd sit in the garden, laughing and joking
With his friend, his family and the sun up above.

But he knows the harsh reality now
After years on the streets and trying to get by.
All he has is his coat and his cap and his sack,
That ragged old man with the sad, lonely eyes.

Emer Tumilty (14)
Sacred Heart Grammar School

WAR

Nation against nation,
State against state,
Campaign to combat
Or to put an end
To something like hate.
War is not necessary. Some people think
It's fun
Until they die like
Everyone.
To wage or carry on war
Has many side effects like death,
Disease or starvation.
So beware, you're not safe. It's always
There behind every lurking corner.
Beware!

Siofra Crozier (14)
Sacred Heart Grammar School

NEW CLOTHES FOR CHRISTMAS

Christmas is coming,
And there is magic in the air,
Everyone thinks of new clothes,
And what they are going to wear.

A new jumper, or perhaps a new coat,
Oh no! in my old clothes I will look a mess,
So I'll have to be good to Mummy,
And just maybe, she'll buy me a new dress.

Louise Byrnes (13)
Sacred Heart Grammar School

SKOOL WAYZ

Uniformed zombies,
Pigtails, curls and tights.
Snot-nosed nit-infested brats
And bloody playground fights.

Wicked English teachers
Armed with rotten, pointy sticks
If they give us one more homework,
Through the window we'll throw bricks.

Greasy dinner ladies
Serving mouldy eggs and chips
With warty, stubby, grotty hands
And filthy fingertips.

Going through this every day,
We kids have got school sussed,
For come the summer holidays,
You won't see us for dust.

Aoife McCoy (13)
Sacred Heart Grammar School

DREAMING!

When I fall asleep at night
a whole new world stands before my eyes.
Where the birds soar high and sing all day,
where the horses stay grazing in the hay.

There's a lovely smell of the freshly cut grass,
the sheep bleat happily in the fields as I pass,
I run through the meadows and swim in the lake.
Is this real or is it fake?

I wake up and wonder
was it a dream?
Dawn has come
and I see the sun gleam!

Ciara McKeown (14)
Sacred Heart Grammar School

CROKE PARK

Oh how I would love to go to Croke Park,
On the third Sunday of September,
To see Armagh take the field by storm,
It's a day I'd always remember.

The atmosphere is electric,
There's a shake in my hand,
As the teams line up,
Behind the Artone Boys' Band.

As they walk round the field,
My heart's in my mouth,
Some people are shouting,
'They'll win, there's no doubt!'

A tough game for all,
But a victory at end,
Kerry with 1-6,
Armagh with 0-10

As we headed for home,
We were all in great cheer,
As the Sam Maguire was coming home,
For the very first year!

Leanne McCoy (13)
Sacred Heart Grammar School

OUTCAST SPIRIT

I sit in front of you yet you do not see
There is no one to care other than me,
I rattle my cup but you do not care
I am an outcast, I'm nearly a scare.

All of you have jobs and families too
You pass with your children saying hastily, 'Shoo,'
And what did I ever do so wrong
To make my clothes tatty and make them pong.

I sleep on the ground which you spit upon
My jar is empty from dusk to dawn,
For those who give me their two ps and ones,
I am grateful and hope they are blessed by the suns.

You pass me by in your fancy cars
Your garden's large and full of beautiful flowers
You do not see the value of you
Of your life, your family, the things that you do.

I have told you now of the way I live
I hope next time you see me you'll willingly give,
For life is precious and not to be rushed
Think of me next time you see a pile of dust.

Kerri Cooper (11)
Sacred Heart Grammar School

THE BLUE POEM

As blue as the oceans
As blue as the seas.
Blue is the perfect colour for me!
The fast flowing rivers,
The shimmering streams,
Blue is a watery colour it seems!

But juicy, ripe blueberries on the thorny bush
Under the baby-blue sky where the clouds all rush
Are more sources of blue,
So please don't forget that
Not all types of blue have to be wet!

Emma McAteer (13)
Sacred Heart Grammar School

ALL MIXED UP!

A simple aim, yet who's to blame.
A complex matter, of which the whole world will shatter.
We're all in this together, will it last forever?
All religions and races
Colours and faces.

Violence was said never to solve anything,
So why keep killing me, you and everything.
Two wrongs don't make a right,
So why do you continue to fight?

While we laugh, talk and dance,
Little Afghan children don't even have a chance.
Why did this happen, what can we do?
With a little encouragement, we can help, yes - me and you!

Parts of families lost, weeping all around,
Some bodies still have to be found.
Fighter planes soaring high up above,
Whatever happened to peace, forgiveness and love?

Billie Phipps-Tyndall (13)
Sacred Heart Grammar School

OUR WORLD TODAY

Green is the grass, blue is the sea.
These are obvious, what else do I see?
I see hatred and pollution,
I see problems, not solutions.
I hear noise and commotion,
Marriages with no devotion.
I see people fighting, here and there.
I see people dying everywhere.
I see barren places,
Where crops don't grow.
A farmer with no money,
And no seeds to sow.
And a little girl,
So very pretty.
An orphan all alone,
In this great city.
With no shoes on her feet
And no food to eat.
She lies here dying,
And though in pain, she isn't crying.
She prayed to God day and night
To keep her going and help her fight.
She prayed all night, she prayed all day,
But one morning, she didn't have anything to say.
She was up in heaven with God, to stay.

Lana Mallon (12)
Sacred Heart Grammar School

LIFE IS UNPREDICTABLE!

One day I sat upon a stool,
And said to myself
'Life is cruel!'
I remembered back
When I fell off my chair,
Everyone suddenly began to stare!
I remember the time,
When I was ten,
I used to have a secret den
But now that I'm too big for that,
It's occupied by the neighbour's cat!
Now that I'm fourteen,
Embarrassments at its peak
I wonder what will happen
To me next week?

Ciara Hughes (14)
Sacred Heart Grammar School

LOVE!

Love is precious,
Love is great,
Love can put you in a state.
It lifts you up when you're feeling down,
Love makes the world go around.
I'm on cloud nine, oh he's so fine,
I talked to him the other day,
But he ignored me and walked away!

Janelle McAteer (13)
Sacred Heart Grammar School

RED

Red are the holly berries
gleaming in the wood,
Red is the breasted robin
in his search for food,
Red is Christmas time
bringing joy to a season so cold,
Red gives rise to visions of warmth
steaming from miner's coal,
Red is the sunset
glowing in lover's hearts,
Red is what they see
as their love drifts apart.
Red for fragrant roses
and peace-loving poppies too,
I couldn't live without red
Could you?

Anna Burke (14)
Sacred Heart Grammar School

AUTUMN

A   tree in all its glory, coloured yellow, gold and red.
U   mbrellas are put up to stop us getting wet.
T   urn back the clocks
U   ntil June comes again.
M   ake sure to wrap up warm
N   ow that autumn's here again!

Bronagh Clarke (14)
Sacred Heart Grammar School

SCREAMS FOR HELP

Two mighty towers,
Come falling, crumbling down.
The painful screams,
The cries for salvation.
Who, who would, who could do such a thing?
America, a bird with a broken wing.
Screeches for help,
How does it recover?
In a brutal way,
Innocent people killed far and wide,
Broken hearts, far and wide.
But there is only one question on everyone's mind.
Why?

Cathy Grant (12)
Sacred Heart Grammar School

INSPIRATION

Inspiration needed
nobody knows its destination
look high, look low
look where it might go.

'But what does it look like?'
I hear you cry.
Is it up there in the sky
Or is it down there where nobody goes.
Or it could be right under your nose.
nobody knows.

No nobody knows.

Claire McMurray (13)
Sacred Heart Grammar School

UNITED WE STAND

A day to remember
The 11th of September
One calculated hour of madness
Plunged the world into sorry, grief and sadness.

This was not fair
They did not care
For wonderful, precious life
What made these terrorists anger, sore in rife?

Why did this happen to our nation?
What must we do to be patient?
Why do these people want a war?
Oh my God, Oh my God, what for?

Our countries must pray for everlasting peace,
Not let these people die in vain, violence must cease.
So united we stand, divided we fall
So please God help us all.

Patrice Byrnes (11)
Sacred Heart Grammar School

QUIET ALL AROUND

Down in the garden near the tree,
Quiet all around.
Not a sound nor moving thing,
Except footsteps on the ground.

I start to run through the street
And quiet is all around.
The trees are swaying in the wind
With a gentle, calming sound.

Near the road, free of cars,
And quiet all around.
And then very suddenly,
I heard a rustling sound.

I run across the road,
And quiet all around.
Then a skid, a bang, a scream . . .
My friend lies on the ground.

Áine Reilly (12)
Sacred Heart Grammar School

PEACE

I had a dream one night:
everyone lived,
everyone loved,
everyone shared,
and everyone cared,
no one was lonely,
and no one was left out.
In my dream, the world was happy
every race, every religion, every colour and every nation.
My dream was a perfect dream,
a dream without fault,
a dream the world did not recognise.
God gave us hope,
and God gave us love,
so let there be peace on Earth,
may the fighting cease and tortures rest
may there be peace on the Earth.

Shellie McKeown (13)
Sacred Heart Grammar School

THE RAINBOW

The rainbow is wonderful
Away up high in the sky.
With its glorious colours
When it starts to die.
The colours are warm
When they start to form.
With its amazing bright colours
But it has to reform.
It comes and goes
Like lightning throes.
Beautiful colours but,
They must go.
The rain has stopped
And the sun will glow
Here comes the night very slow
Brown and yellow, it's like a scene.

Emma O'Gorman
Sacred Heart Grammar School

MY PET

My pet is a cat
My pet is never off her mat
My pet is fluffy
My pet is called Muffy
My pet is boring
My pet is . . . oh my
My pet is dead!

Sarah Connolly (12)
Sacred Heart Grammar School

THE MOON

Falling rain, wind and hail, another rotten night!
Raindrops dance beneath the street light
To fall on car windscreens and sparkle so bright.
Suddenly a break in the clouds, the full moon in sight.
Like a flick of a switch the town comes to life.
A silvery moon cuts through darkness like a knife.
Down cobbled streets this yellow brick road
On factory walls like a spotlight showed.
Stray cats and dogs leave shelters dry
To feed on chip shop leftovers from passers-by.
As most sleep, a silence descends on the early hours
And moonlight disappears, replaced by the dawn sun's powers.

Nikki Larkin (14)
Sacred Heart Grammar School

WINTER

Winter is fun,
Winter is snowy,
Winter is cold,
It can be blowy.

The sun stays away,
But may come out another day
The snowmen will melt and say goodbye
And the children will try not to cry.

It will start to get hot again,
And children can play lots of games.

Corinne Jordan (13)
Sacred Heart Grammar School

HALLOWE'EN

Bonfires crackling,
Witches cackling.
Vampires are out,
And bats are about.
This night we call Hallowe'en,
Is the night spirits can be seen.
Children are playing,
And they are saying,
Trick or treat, trick or treat,
Give us something nice to eat.
Witches, bats they're scared of
Nothing, until midnight strikes.
Whoosh! Bang! Whoosh! Bang!
Fireworks are set.
Now their trousers are wet.

Katie McGovern (11)
Sacred Heart Grammar School

I WONDER?

War and death go hand in hand,
It adds suffering to many a land.
I wonder, do world leaders care?
Creating havoc and despair.
Mothers, fathers, children dead,
No one left to use the bed.
Homes destroyed, families broken,
Some are left just hoping.
Bombs worth millions, to kill and maim.
I wonder, what is the gain
In all this hunger, suffering and pain?

Niamh D'Arcy (12)
Sacred Heart Grammar School

GOLD

The golden cat lazes in the golden sun
Yawning in the midday heat
Paws for thought as he totters along
To find the noise of a little gold mouse.

Glistening sun turns to shining moon
When the night comes out,
With the shimmering stars and the golden moon
Shining in the darkening skies.
The little gold mouse scampers along
Into a hole and to no harm.
The cat runs by with no idea.
As the skies darken more,
Home gets more clear.

Sarah-Louise O'Hare (14)
Sacred Heart Grammar School

AUTUMN

The autumn leaves are
Falling down, down, down
Red, yellow and brown.

Gracefully swirling
Tracing the air as they fall

As farmers and
Children gather
Us in stacks.

We scream . . .
There's no
Turning back.

Vicki Lennon (12)
Sacred Heart Grammar School

IN THE BLACK OF NIGHT

It's midnight in the wild, wild west
I lift my head from its place of rest
To see the immobile sillote
Of a glossy horse soaked in sweat.

The horse is black with a white blaze
I can see it clearly from the window where I gaze
Its mane and tail look sliver in this light
I can see its muscular body as it gallops through the night.

Many a man has tried to tame
This horse I can see through my windowpane.
It's a mystery known only by the sunlight, moon and stars
How often it travels and how far?

Sarah Garvey (13)
Sacred Heart Grammar School

MY GRANNY

My granny is the best,
She's better than the rest,
She takes me everywhere,
And lets me know she cares.

She takes me to the swimming pool
Which is far, far better than school,
She buys me everything,
And takes me to the choir to sing.

I love my granny very much,
And tell her with a loving clutch,
I see her every day,
'God don't let her die,' I pray.

Ciara Higgins (13)
Sacred Heart Grammar School

AUTUMN

Autumn, the most colourful season,
all the leaves forming a carpet of colour on park paths.

Autumn, the cold weather is creeping near.
Mist is falling like a blanket of silk across the land.
The moon glows brighter than ever in which scenes
are chilled feelings in the air.

Autumn, time of harvest
and the trees and bushes blooming with berries.

All these things come into only one season and that's
Autumn.

Claire McAteer (11)
Sacred Heart Grammar School

LOVER'S VOWS

I love you, you love me,
It's really not so hard to see,
You're the one that I need
When I cry and when I bleed.

When you're sad and full of fear,
I'm the one who's always here,
Through the day and through the night,
I'll always make sure that you're alright.

All the way from June to May,
You know my love will always stay.
It has to be said, that it's oh so true,
That you love me and I love you.

Kelly Savage (14)
Sacred Heart Grammar School

MY DOG

My dog's name is Floppy
He loves flowers, especially a poppy

He's brown and white
But he would never bite

He is a basset hound
But he's never been to the pound

He has got bit flat paws
And almost no claws

He's got a big, long nose
And a very posh, little pose

He has got big, droopy eyes
And snaps at any flies

His ears are so big
And he really likes to dig

His body is really long
And when he's wet he has a bit of a pong

So that's what my dog is like.

Siofra Gough (11)
Sacred Heart Grammar School

FREEDOM

My spirit is free
My body not
I see you bustle round my stable
Tie my lead rope in a knot
Should I stay?
Or should I go?

As you give me my hay
I think to myself
I will stay
because friendship pays more
Than freedom would pay.

Ruth Graham (12)
Sacred Heart Grammar School

MY LITTLE SISTER!

My sister's name is Emily,
She's sometimes singing merrily.
But other times she's bold and rude,
And some of the time she's a cool dude.

She's only three years old you see,
And sometimes really bad to me.
When she goes in a huff,
She sits in the corner, 'Puff, puff, puff!'

When she's in a good mood,
She sits and eats all her food.
And also lets me do her hair,
So when I pull, she isn't a bear.

When she's good I like her a lot,
But when she's bad I wish she'd rot.
She always shares her sweets with me
And I really love her deeply.

Clare Grant (11)
Sacred Heart Grammar School

WEEKENDS

Everybody loves weekends,
And I'm sure we all know why
It's a time to go out with your friends
And lie in until half-past five.

On Friday night the fun begins
I have a great time with all my friends
Our parents don't know what time we'll get in
But we know the fun will never end.

On Saturday I lie in till three
I'm really glad it's two days till Monday
I lie with my blanket in front of the TV
I wish I could stay like this all day.

Sundays I really don't like that much
Because tomorrow I know what day it is
I have piles of homework I haven't touched
Why does the weekend go by in a whizz.

Róisín Murphy (14)
Sacred Heart Grammar School

MY GRANNY

There's a special place I like to go,
Especially when I'm feeling low.
That special place is my granny's home,
And she's the reason I write this poem.

She laughs, she jokes, she cooks a great meal
In my life she means a great deal.
When I'm feeling low she lifts me high,
We are great friends, my granny and I.

Lisa Hamill (11)
Sacred Heart Grammar School

A Day In The Life Of A Tennis Ball

I'm all alone in my cupboard
Darkness is all I can see
The Hoover's the only thing here
And it doesn't seem to like me.

Oh look, the cupboard is open
I can see light through the door
Michael's picking me up
And bouncing me on the floor.

I'm on the tennis court
With Michael and his dad
All they're doing is bouncing me
And it's starting to make me mad.

I'm back in the cupboard
All on my own
I'd rather be bounced
Than sit here alone.

Lucy O'Hare (11)
Sacred Heart Grammar School

Snow White

She falls over mountains, lakes and everything she sees,
On her way making everything a white, fluffy fleece,
A white house with a white chimney and a white roof,
In white fields, white horses with white hooves.
White cars, on white roads in the white city,
White birds sleep on a branch on the white tree,
Snow White is the only thing that passes the street.

Adele Cunningham (13)
Sacred Heart Grammar School

THE WATERFALL

It rushes by without a care,
By the insects, birds and bears.
No one will stand in the way
Of the mighty river Sway.
Ask him 'Where are you going?'
But no answer is given.
The water steadily heads
To the drop ahead,
No hesitation, no pause,
Over the edge, to the next stage.
Where boulders and rocks,
Will roughen the path
You can try but no one
Will stand in the way
Or the mighty river Sway!

Delia Paxton (14)
Sacred Heart Grammar School

A SPRING MORNING

I woke up early one April morning,
I put on my coat and went outside.
A light breeze was blowing and the fog covered the hills.

The trees swayed gently from side to side,
The flowers danced among the grass
And rabbits hopped from field to field.

The birds chirped and the sea swept to and fro
All my troubles were forgotten and I closed my eyes
And thought of wonderful things.

It was wonderful . . . simply wonderful.

Jennifer Maguire (11)
Sacred Heart Grammar School

RAIN

Rain, rain, rain
Oh what a pain
It's raining again
Let's go out
'Wellies on,' we shout
As we splish, splash
In puddles galore
'Get out of the rain,'
My mummy roars
Her fists are clenched
For we are happily drenched
Soaked to the skin
And safely in
Rain, rain, rain
Come again.

Cecilia McSweeney (11)
Sacred Heart Grammar School

IN THE DARK

Walking in the dark at night
Shadows behind fill me with fright.
Owls hoot overhead
I wish I was at home all snug in bed.
In the bushes is someone peeping?
Is the witch awake or sleeping?
Is someone stalking me?
All these thoughts make me flee.
Puffing and panting, I arrive at the door
My fears of the dark are with me no more.

Leah McGuinness (11)
Sacred Heart Grammar School

I WISH I WAS ...

I wish I was a bird so high in the sky,
Getting around by being able to fly.

I wish I was a snake slithering around,
Hissing and sissing on the dusty ground.

I wish I was a fish in the deep blue sea,
Swimming around just my friends and me.

I wish I was a tiger hunting my prey,
Eating more and more animals day after day.

I wish I was a duck in the small pond,
People throwing bread to me, all day long.

I wish I was a horse that lived in a field,
Going to competitions, winning cups and shields.

I wish I was a spider in my web,
Eating the flies, when they were all dead.

I wish I was the biggest animal
I think you can see
But that won't happen, because I'm just plain old *me!*

Tara Crilly (11)
Sacred Heart Grammar School

THE SUN

The sunrise shines like gold,
It delicately shimmers like a diamond
And lights up the path of travelling trespassers
Birds perch between trees
And gaze deeply at this delightful image.

When the sunset appears
All warmth is lost
Animals are troubled and
Scamper to make their way to their tunnels
Some are blinded by this light
Yet, some blissfully enjoy this new awakening.

Claire O'Donnell
Sacred Heart Grammar School

MY TURN TO DANCE

As I enter the hall
There they stand on stage,
Very straight and tall.
The accordion starts to play
As they nervously wait,
Then off they go on their way.

Hopping, skipping and jumping
Swirling and twirling round and round,
The hearts of the dancers pumping.
Legs out straight, feet crossed
As they cover the stage
Each with their hair tossed.

The brightly coloured dresses
Glittering and sparkling in the light
On those girls with the perfectly curled tresses.
The adjudicator rings the bell,
Oh no, it's my turn,
Now let's hope I do well.

Naoise Curran (12)
Sacred Heart Grammar School

THE WALK

One day as I was walking
Just as I normally do,
Down to the shop
To get my daily fix of sweets.
I noticed something a bit strange
Nothing strange ever happened to me,
But I knew someone or something was watching me.

I was scared and alone.
I walked faster,
But it walked faster.
I ran,
But it ran.
I stopped,
But it stopped.
I crossed the road,
But it was still there
I couldn't get away.
It wasn't an animal or the wind,
Was it my imagination?
No. It was . . .
It was my conscience,
It had caught up on me
Slowly, creeping
I still couldn't get away.

All those lies, all those rumours came back to me
And I didn't feel so good.
I didn't know how to handle that feeling,
So I didn't.

Helen McAvoy (14)
Sacred Heart Grammar School

BEDTIME

Oh Ma, please!
Dad said to ask you,
Just another half hour,
Till this programme is through.

This isn't fair,
I'm the eldest after all,
Maybe I'll sneak down,
And watch from the hall.

They don't understand,
Or maybe don't care,
They still treat me
As though I am only four.

My bedtime's too early,
At this rate, I can see,
I'll still be put to bed early
When I'm thirty three.

Carol Duffy (11)
Sacred Heart Grammar School

THE WOMAN NEXT DOOR

The woman next door is set in her ways
She works all day but seldom plays.
Kind and gentle to her flowers in their bed,
To her plants and her trees it has to be said.
Her dogs and her cats roam freely each day
her birds in her trees always seem to stay
But very few callers from morn until night
It's the woman next door with so much delight.

Laura Fitzpatrick (11)
Sacred Heart Grammar School

THAT TIME OF THE YEAR

Christmas time and its rush, rush, rush,
The people in the queue push, push, push,
The prices are outrageously high,
Stress levels reaching the sky.

I've already been to all the shops,
Up and down the lift,
But nowhere can I find the perfect gift,
I've had enough - I don't care
I'll just pick up something from anywhere.

Get home with feet blistered and sore,
Cranky and tired I rush through the door,
It's the children all this fuss is for,
But when you see their faces on Christmas Day
You know you wouldn't want it any other way.

Shóna McConville (13)
Sacred Heart Grammar School

CATS

Cats are fluffy,
Cats are cute,
I just love them what can I do?

Cats are lovely,
Cats are kind,
My four are never off my mind.

Mine are white and fluffy,
Whilst the others are black and funky.

Claudia Cole (11)
Sacred Heart Grammar School

THE STORM

The thunder roared and the lightning struck
The rain it did pour on that cold December night
In the dark bedroom where shadows flickered on the wall
Paul twisted and turned in his small bed.

The windows rattled and the doors creaked
But still Paul could not sleep.
But it wasn't the howling wind or crashing thunder
That was keeping Paul awake, for it was a tiny mouse
In the corner of his room and it was chanting:
    'So you see,' began the mouse
    'It was not the wind or the rain
    That was keeping you awake
    But it was tiny little *me!'*

Éadaoin Hynes (12)
Sacred Heart Grammar School

HALLOWE'EN!

Hallowe'en, Hallowe'en
Only witches to be seen!

Scary nights
And plenty of frights

Fireworks ablaze
Little children totally agaze.

Knocks on doors for trick or treat
Apples, nuts, crisps and hopefully a sweet.

Hallowe'en, Hallowe'en
Soon the witches will not be seen!

Ciara Monaghan (11)
Sacred Heart Grammar School

FLOWERS

Red is the rose
That in my garden grows
A warm-hearted flower
A flower of love

Fair is the lily
Which flourishes in the valley
Snow-white in colour
But a rainbow of soul.

Dainty is the daisy
Yellow and white
Beautiful colours
What a sight.

Delicate is the daffodil
That grows beside my wall
Common, but gorgeous
My favourite of all.

Emma Madine (14)
Sacred Heart Grammar School

MY CATS

I really have such lovely pets,
Without them I would really fret.
They are my company when I'm lonely,
And so I love them truly, only.

In the mornings off they roam,
When I come back they come home.
They are the most lovely cats,
And they're great at catching rats.

They all rush over just to eat,
Then they go and rest their feet.
The mother treats them with a lick,
The tom treats them with a kick.

When night comes round,
They can't be found.
But by morning they are there,
To greet the day bright and fair.

Bronagh Fitzpatrick (11)
Sacred Heart Grammar School

MY PUPPY

My puppy is cute and very small
She jumps up on you, but she's not bad at all

She is only six months old
And sometimes does what she is told.

We did manage to succeed
In getting her to fetch her lead

And we taught her how to 'Sit'
But that's about it!

She enjoys a little treat
And will happily lick your feet

She loves going on walks
And little birds she stalks

Lucy is coloured black and tan
And I am her biggest fan.

Niamh Montgomery (12)
Sacred Heart Grammar School

THE LITTLE SQUIRREL

Once upon an autumn night
There sat a squirrel in its delight.
For over there, all the squirrel could see
Was a pile of nuts, the squirrel was filled with glee.
No more looking for food in the cold,
Now he could get back to his cosy, warm hole
And sleep in there until the winter is gone.
Then the squirrel began to sing his own special song
As he rolled each nut down into his hole
He wondered, from who had the nuts been stolen?
'I hope they don't find out it was me.'
That naughty little squirrel thought anxiously.
Soon there was a bang at the door
And papa squirrel entered with an angry face.
Little squirrel knew he had been disgraced
For all that the poor little squirrel had proved
Is that other people's things should *not be moved!*

Sarah Casey (11)
Sacred Heart Grammar School

MY ELEPHANT

Did you know I had a pet elephant?
He is big and heavy and rough,
Elephant does things that I can't,
He's definitely strong and tough.

We went down the street for a walk,
Of course I was on his big back,
We pounded the road and I waved to my friends,
It really was good crack.

I decided he should be in the zoo,
With others the same as himself,
So I said goodbye and had a wee cry,
And bought a toy one instead for my shelf.

Shauna Reeves (11)
Sacred Heart Grammar School

SUMMER

Golden sun in the sky,
Fluffy clouds floating by.
Windsurfing looks such fun,
But I prefer to lie in the sun.

Hamburgers are so very nice,
With drinks as cold as ice.
Cold lollies are tasty too,
Ice creams dripping on my shoe.

Birds singing a sweet song,
Laughing children all day long.
Sausages sizzling on the pan,
The crunching of the golden sand.

Pain of sunburn on my nose,
Seaweed tangles between my toes.
Chilly water passes me by,
But I'm on my lilo so all day I lie.

Smell of the salty sea,
And of barbecue so smoky.
Scent of flower such a pleasant smell
Summer I love so well.

Fionnuala Haughey (12)
Sacred Heart Grammar School

THE COMPETITION

The tension was rising, the hall was filling
And there I was ready to do my singing.

I stood in front of the judge's desk,
And braced myself for this nerve-racking test.
I opened my mouth, but no sound came out
And there and then I began to doubt.

'Will I be able to sing my best,
Or will all these people jeer and jest?'
Out of my mouth came a stutter and stammer
And I began to sweat in an unladylike manner.

The judge said, 'In your own time,'
But all I could do was rhyme and mime,
The words of that song I knew so well
But my confidence just fell and fell.

Finally I said, 'I just can't do it.'
And I was out of that hall as fast as a bullet.
My mum asked, 'How did it go, please tell?'
Let's just say, it didn't go well.

Maria Dobbin (13)
Sacred Heart Grammar School

THE RAINBOW

The rainbow is so beautiful
The colours are so bright,
If you look high up at it
it is a wonderful sight.

After a sun shower
The rainbow will appear,
It seems as if you can touch it
It seems like it's so near.

There are lots of fables in our land
And one that I've been told,
Is that at the end of it you would see
A tiny, little leprechaun and a pot of gold.

Rachel Gribben (11)
Sacred Heart Grammar School

THE FUTURE

What will happen in the future?
Nobody knows.
We'll just have to wait
And see how it goes.

Will we have cars that can fly?
Will we have cars at all?
Will our houses
Still be made of walls?

Will we have to go to school?
Or will we learn from home?
Being given our homework
By mobile phone.

Will we find out the answers,
To these questions soon?
You never know,
By then, we could be living on the moon.

Siobhan Ruck (11)
Sacred Heart Grammar School

AUTUMN

Leaves, leaves make me sneeze
Especially in the autumn breeze.

When I see the squirrel
Climbing up the tree,
I think maybe
He's gathering nuts for you and me.

Every day I hear leaves say,
'Crunch, crunch, crunch.'
Before I go for my
Lunch, lunch, lunch.

But what I like most to do
Is: fall to my knees
Right in the middle
Of all those leaves!

Amy Lavery (11)
Sacred Heart Grammar School

WITCHES

We come at the dead of night,
Us three, we come to give you a fright.
We work our spell and to you we tell
Our horrible words and curses.

We want you to die, die, die,
We want to make you cry, cry, cry.
We are witches, tall and strong
We can make things go horribly wrong.

Keren Larkin (12)
Sacred Heart Grammar School

HALLOWE'EN

On the night of Hallowe'en
A story can be told
As people sit around
A huge fire chatting and laughing.

But on the night
On a haunted hill
Four witches stand
Casting a spell mumbling and chanting
They stop! Total silence.

Suddenly they let out a wicked laugh
But watch out, because that spell might be cast.
On you!

Catherine Hughes (11)
Sacred Heart Grammar School

ANGELS!

Are angels really up there?
I wondered one day.
Above the bright blue sky, far, far away!

Do they really keep us safe
And protect us day and night?
Or is it all a fantasy, some day we will see?

Have angels never told a lie,
Or are they just special
Because God has chosen them to be the one to protect me!

Alana Carroll (12)
Sacred Heart Grammar School

WALKING HOME FROM SCHOOL

With scarcely one mile from the school to my home,
When no one collects me I go it alone,
Alone with my thoughts, the birds and the bees,
The short stretch of village, the road flanked with trees.
Free from the classroom, the din and the talk,
My mind goes amitching as homeward I walk.

Turning the corner I see old Pat O'Hare
Sitting alone now, too big for his chair.
His dark eyes meet mine with a soft, gentle glow,
Betraying a wisdom that I'll never know.
'And what did you learn at school, my child?'
'Computer loading systems, the internet guide.'

How thoughtless of me to answer like that,
Flaunting a language unknown to old Pat!
He furrows his forehead, his dark eyes look sad,
Perhaps he's recalling when he was a lad.
I move along grieved by the graces I lack,
The village grows smaller each time I look back.

Once more on my own, I'm thinking, I'm focused,
I'm seeing, I'm hearing the things seldom noticed.
A young wasp zooms past in bright coloured vest
Then chooses a flower where it snatches a rest.
And somewhere above me, in the arms of a tree,
A blackbird is singing her heart out to me.

On the stone bridge I ponder, as I dangle my feet,
And gaze at the river where earth and sky meet.
Today I've learned lessons no textbook can teach,
Pearls of wisdom that seemed out of reach.
The hedgerows, the creatures, the streamlets so cool
All mint their own magic as I walk home from school.

Claire Rooney (11)
Sacred Heart Grammar School

WHY DOES IT ALWAYS RAIN?

Dark clouds, always in the sky
Puddles everywhere
The weathermen always seem to lie,
It just doesn't seem fair.

Drip, drop down my window
Will it ever stop?
The temperature's are low,
Why can't it be hot?

I always hate to see the rain
Nothing ever to do,
Oh, I'd love to be in Spain
The rain is never due.

Elizabeth O'Hanlon (13)
Sacred Heart Grammar School

AN ANGEL

An angel, do you have one close by?
An angel, there for when you cry,
An angel, to make your tears dry.

When you're feeling sad,
When you're days seem bad,
When everything makes you mad;

Think an angel, always to care,
Think an angel, always there,
Think an angel, an angel for Clare!

Clare Campbell (13)
Sacred Heart Grammar School

Up In The Attic . . .

Up in the attic from behind the toys
There comes a loud, groaning noise,
Could it be mice or rats
Birds, bugs or bats?

There are lots of strange creatures
With really weird features,
Like their twelve wriggly toes
And a wonky nose.

Do they have yellow and green skin
And a big, spotty chin?
Does each have six googly eyes
And are they big in size?

I think they're lonely and shy
Because I've heard them sob and cry,
I'd like to be friends
But I might meet my end.

I think I'll go near
But I'm shaking with fear.

Dominique French (13)
Sacred Heart Grammar School

My Cats

During the day
My cats play and play,
In the sun they lie
Watching the day go by.
If you open the door
They dash in and slip across the wooden floor.

But by night
They stalk other animals giving them a fright,
I often think of them when I'm in bed
And hope that because of them other little animals aren't dead
But I know in the morning they'll be waiting for me
And when I see them I'll fill up with glee!

Nicola McNally (12)
Sacred Heart Grammar School

SCHOOL IS BORING!

School is boring
Oh yes it is
Sitting in a classroom
Listening to teachers go on and on
About stuff that is pointless.
Why can't they make school somewhere fun?
Somewhere that gives you great pleasure to go to?
I would love school to be a big fairground
With loads of giant roller coasters and dodgems
And if they really want us to go to boring old school
Why don't they cut it down to twice a week?
Or even better, once a week?
It's impossible to understand.
And homework, I mean, we sit and work hard all day,
And as if that's not enough, they give us work to do at home as well!
When I grow up, I'm going to ban all forms of education,
because, *I hate school!*

Caitriona Gormley (11)
Sacred Heart Grammar School

MY DOG

My dog is white and fluffy,
And is always getting very scruffy.

He sleeps at the end of my bed at night,
And by barking at people he gives them a fright.

He rolls in the muck all day,
And is always wanting to play.

He constantly wants to be fed,
And if we give him too much, he will be sick on my bed.

He is cute, but annoying and he gets on my nerves,
But when I wake in the morning, he is still always there.
I love him.

Claire Malone (11)
Sacred Heart Grammar School

DESTRUCTION

On September eleventh
As the world gazed in horror
I feared to think
What lurks in minds
So evil and callous
As to plot the destruction
Of a city
And its people.

Cathy McAlinden (13)
Sacred Heart Grammar School

THE CARNIVAL

People rushing everywhere
It's six o'clock, let's go to the fair.
Children screaming with delight
As the dodgems go bump in the night.

Fireworks exploding with wonderful sights
Children amazed by these colourful lights.
While the Ferris wheel goes round and round
The tin cans come tumbling down.

The Terminator, with people on it,
'Oh no, run, they're going to vomit!'
Time to move on to the merry-go-round
Children are crying, 'Let me down.'

Two days have passed, the carnival closes
All rides are half price and everyone knows this.
As we say goodbye to the fair
I'm going home happy, with a big, cuddly bear.

Louise O'Hanlon (11)
Sacred Heart Grammar School

HALLOWE'EN

Hallowe'en is spooky, Hallowe'en is fun,
You can go freely to play tricks on everyone,
Here's another great advantage, that sends children wild,
Getting a week off school is great especially to a child.

On Hallowe'en night fireworks blaze so bright,
It is wonderful to watch, in the starlight,
But be careful if you have a pet,
You don't want to send it to the vet.

Grace Cole (11)
Sacred Heart Grammar School

MY BEST FRIEND

She was there when no one was,
I filled her in with all the buzz.
She is really a cool crack,
She would often offer me a Tic-Tac.

We sit beside each other all the time
She tells me about the boys who are fine.
I would help her with her maths
She guides me in all the right paths.

We sometimes fight,
But it will soon be put right.
She always has a smile on her face,
As a friend she is ace.

We go shopping down the town
We both support County Down.
We get on so well
We will be friends forever that you can tell.

Niamh Haughey (12)
Sacred Heart Grammar School

SLEEPOVERS

Sleepovers are really cool
You always break a stool
On that night you don't get to sleep
Everyone ends up counting sheep.

The next day you go down the street
And shop till you drop, right off your feet
Into a restaurant for some food
Then back down town, a real cool dude.

I hope everyone had a real, super day
I only wished that everyone could stay
It's all over now, there's homework to do
Oh my goodness, the time just flew!

Alannah White (11)
Sacred Heart Grammar School

THE TRAGEDY OF NEW YORK

Whilst watching the news late last night,
I couldn't believe what I saw,
Destruction and violence,
It looked like the start of a war.

Buildings crumbling all around,
There was smoke and fire everywhere,
Some evil terrorists had hijacked two planes,
And crashed them without a care.

The city was in a panic,
Bodies lay all around,
There were so many casualties and blood,
You couldn't see the ground.

So many innocent lives were taken,
Death was in the air,
Babies crying, screams of terror,
And all I could do was stare.

Danielle Rooney (12)
Sacred Heart Grammar School

THE EYES OF THE NIGHT

How they shine so bright
Blinking in the moonlight
Winking down at the world
From the black that is the night.

How they light up the dark
By glittering oh so bright
How I love to see them
To see the stars at night.

Sometimes they are falling
Like teardrops from the sky
Falling from the sky at night
Like teardrops from my eye.

But when they disappear
And the sun appears in the sky
I just picture those shining eyes
The shining eyes of the night.

Yvonne Smyth (13)
Sacred Heart Grammar School

HALLOWE'EN

The bonfire's flames dancing bright
Glowing amber and red in the night
Roaring and crackling of the burning pile
This fire should last quite a while.

The children squeal and run along
With painted faces and costumes on
The fireworks whistle, bang and glow
As they shoot up to and fro.

Bob the apple and trick or treat
A few of the games we play when we meet
Crisps and nuts, chocolate and sweets
These are the goodies that we eat.

Nicola Mullan (11)
Sacred Heart Grammar School

AUTUMN'S CHARMS

Autumn is here once again,
With colours bright and bold.
The nights get shorter, the mornings don't remain,
Now all we need is our fires full of coal.

Fields are full with pumpkins round,
The crops are just collected,
Cobs of corn lie on the ground,
It is time for summer to be rejected.

When the sun is setting in the vale,
Whilst squirrels busy themselves making a bed,
The storm has started, the gale has arrived,
The leaves of the trees have fallen upon the old, hay shed.
Autumn is here for another three months,
So enjoy it as much as you can!

Teresa Quinn (11)
Sacred Heart Grammar School

HIJACKED!

I can't stay long
Not today
Not ever
Please don't cry I will be with you forever.

Don't worry about our children
It will be a quick death
They say they want their daddy
Tell me what should I do?

Oh I wish you could have answered your phone
Just to hear your voice one more time
But at least I've got memories of you in my mind.

We live in a very cruel world
Today will be the worst
Planes will hit buildings of great importance
And thousands will be lost.

Get out of that tower
As fast as you can
Or else another life shall be taken
And there shall be no father to hold my baby's hand.

Brian and Anna don't know what's coming
If only God could save the day
They say they love you and miss you
And can't wait to see you again.

Say goodbye to my family and friends too
And let them know I'll always look after them
And love them so.

Five minutes I've got left before my time is up
Remember me always, our love shall never die.
We're about to hit my love
Goodbye.

Ruth Morris (12)
Sacred Heart Grammar School

THE CLOWN

Mad shoes,
Silly tricks,
Wacky clothes,
Big nose.

Laughing, joking
All the time,
Tell a poem,
Do a mime.

Silly clowns,
They are such fun,
At the circus,
You should come!

From now on,
Try not to frown,
Be happy and joyful,
Like the clown!

Claire Durkan (12)
Sacred Heart Grammar School

WHY?

Why does the world go round?
Why does anything make a sound?
Why is the sky blue?
Why do people get the flu?

Why is there war?
Why is an injury sore?
Why is the grass green?
Why are some people very mean?

Why can we see?
Why doesn't everyone know me?
Why do we live in a house?
Why can't I turn into a mouse?

Why is there light?
Why is there night?
Why is there day?
Why do people sit and pray?

Why do we live?
Why do people give?
Why do we die?
Why do some people lie?

Why does a bird fly?
Why does it fly up so high?
Why does the sun shine?
Why can't everything be mine?

Jaimie Bishop (12)
Sacred Heart Grammar School

THE FAMINE

The famine was a time of great starvation,
Harvests of spuds failed the nation.
Every stalk was covered with blight
Families for their lives did fight
For during the famine fever broke out,
It killed people all about
Children in their cots did cry
Men and women said goodbye
They went in boats to the USA
To find work to keep them on their way
Year after year the famine went on
Till nearly all in Ireland were gone
When John Clarke who had great foresight
Discovered a potato resistant to blight.

Susan Cull (12)
Sacred Heart Grammar School

AUTUMN

Autumn is here at last
I can't believe summer has past
All the beautiful leaves are falling
I can hear the wind calling.

The long days have gone away
We can go out in the leaves and play
We can play all day
And go on our way.

It has started to get very cold
The wind has started to get very bold
There is no reason
But we may welcome in the new season.

Caoimhe Quinn (11)
Sacred Heart Grammar School

HALLOWE'EN

It's Hallowe'en, it's the time of the year,
For fun, parties, fireworks and fear.
The night is dark, the sky is bright,
As the flames and the fireworks give out light.

The children dress up as witches or ghosts,
To see who can scare the people the most.
They go around the doors and trick or treat,
Hoping to be handed some money or a sweet.

By the end of the night the flames are out,
Everywhere is quiet and there's no one about.
The children are in their bed fast asleep,
There is no sound, no even a peep.

Aoibheann Doyle (12)
Sacred Heart Grammar School

MY BEST FRIEND

My best friend is tall
While on the other hand I'm quite small.

Her skin is fair
While I'm dark with black hair.

She likes talking
While I love walking.

She loves Spain
While I love the rain.

I wonder what is the same . . .
Oh yea, it's our name.
Niamh!

Niamh McCartan (12)
Sacred Heart Grammar School

My Pony

This July just two months ago
A pony came the colour of snow.

I ran outside to see the surprise
and there he was right before my eyes.

I saddled him up and took him out,
then went for a trot around and about.

He was the slowest pony that ever was seen,
but up on his back I felt like a queen.

As the weeks went by he became a good friend,
I'm sure he'll be faithful right to the end.

The pony that came just two months ago,
the pony the colour, the colour of snow.

Jane Doran (12)
Sacred Heart Grammar School

Hallowe'en Night

It's a cold and dark part of the week
Children are out for trick or treat.
Fireworks bang and light up the night
Masks and costumes to give you a fright.

Bonfires are built higher and higher
Wood and tyres are part of the fire
Witches and ghosts can be seen
It's scary, it's spooky, it's Hallowe'en!

Ciara Tumilty (12)
Sacred Heart Grammar School

HALLOWE'EN

Children go out to trick or treat,
Wondering what they will meet.
The time for ghosts, witches and fear,
Cause Hallowe'en comes just once a year.

'Trick or treat,' the children say,
'Give us something if you may.'
They all go out to have fun,
Brothers, sisters, parents, everyone.

Children get to stay out late,
And the parties are just great.
So on Hallowe'en have some fun,
Eat sweets, pies and a bun,
Yum, yum, yum.

Gemma Small (12)
Sacred Heart Grammar School

AUTUMN

Autumn is the time of year
When I think leaves should start to fear
As it would be getting very chilly
And they would be stood on very shrilly
So autumn is the time of year
When I think leaves should start to fear
As they hear the crisp, crackling sound
As they get stamped to the horrid ground.

Mairead Duffy (11)
Sacred Heart Grammar School